Assessment & Practice
Part 2 of 2
7.2

Contents

JUMP Math
One Yonge Street, Suite 1014
Toronto, Ontario M5E 1E5
Canada
www.jumpmath.org

Writers: Dr. Heather Betel, Dr. Francisco Kibedi, Dr. Anna Klebanov, Julie Lorinc, Saverio Mercurio, Dr. Sohrab Rahbar
Editors: Megan Burns, Liane Tsui, Natalie Francis, Lindsay Karpenko, Margaret Hoogeveen
Layout and Illustrations: Linh Lam, Sawyer Paul, Gabriella Kerr, Huy Lam
Cover Design: Linh Lam, based on an original design by Blakeley Words+Pictures (2014)
Cover Photograph: © Kerrick/iStockphoto

ISBN 978-1-77395-180-5

First printing November 2022

Printed and bound in Canada

Welcome to JUMP Math

Entering the world of JUMP Math means believing that every child has the capacity to be fully numerate and to love math. Founder and mathematician John Mighton has used this premise to develop his innovative teaching method. The resulting resources isolate and describe concepts so clearly and incrementally that everyone can understand them.

JUMP Math is comprised of Teacher Resources, Digital Lesson Slides, student Assessment & Practice Books, assessment tools, outreach programs, and professional development. All of this is presented on the JUMP Math website: **www.jumpmath.org**.

The Teacher Resource is available on the website for free use. Read the introduction to the Teacher Resource before you begin using these materials. This will ensure that you understand both the philosophy and the methodology of JUMP Math. The Assessment & Practice Books are designed for use by students, with adult guidance. Each student will have unique needs and it is important to provide the student with the appropriate support and encouragement as they work through the material.

Allow students to discover the concepts by themselves as much as possible. Mathematical discoveries can be made in small, incremental steps. The discovery of a new step is like untangling the parts of a puzzle. It is exciting and rewarding.

Students will need to answer the questions marked with a [notebook icon] in a notebook. Grid paper notebooks should always be on hand for answering extra questions or when additional room for calculation is needed.

Contents

Unit 4: Number: Fractions

Unit 5: Shape and Space: Transformations

Unit 6: Number: Decimals

PART 2

Unit 7: Patterns and Relations: Equations

Unit 8: Shape and Space: Area

Unit 9: Number: Fractions, Decimals, and Percentages

Unit 10: Statistics and Probability: Probability

Unit 11: Shape and Space: Constructions

Unit 12: Statistics and Probability: Data

Unit 13: Shape and Space: Volume

PR7-10 Analyzing Expressions and Equations

REMINDER: An equation contains an equal sign, while an expression does not. An expression represents a numerical value. An equation represents a statement of equality.

1. Circle the equations. Underline the expressions.

$5n - 3$ $n + 6 > 7$ $7 + 3n$ $7 + 3n = 5 + 2n$ $a + b \leq 4$

$a + b = 4(b + a)$ $8 - 3n = 5$ $a \times b = b \times a$ $4 + 6n - 5m$ $4 + 6n = 5m$

2. What is the same about expressions and equations?

3. How are expressions different from equations?

4. Write an equation that contains the expression $5n + 3$. _____

5. Substitute the given values for the variables and evaluate the expression.

a) $6x - 59$, $x = 7$
   $= 6(7) - 59$
   $= 42 - 59$
   $= -17$

b) $-15 + 3n$, $n = 25$

c) $10d - g$, $g = -11$, $d = 7$

6. Substitute the value for the variable. Is the equation true or false?

a) $5x - 10 = 44$, $x = 11$
   $5(11) - 10 = 44$
   $55 - 10 = 44$
   $45 = 44$, false

b) $25b + 30 = 120$, $b = 4$

c) $210 = 90 + 6p$, $p = 20$

In an expression or equation, a quantity with a variable is called a **variable term** while a quantity without a variable is called a **constant term**.

variable term is $-5x$

$-5x + 13$

constant term is $+13$

The value of the variable term changes depending on the value of the variable.

The constant term is always the same, no matter what the value of the variable is.

7. Complete the table.

	Expression or Equation	Variable Terms	Constant Terms
a)	$-15 + 1y = -3x + 0$	$+1y, -3x$	$-15, 0$
b)	$19m + 18 - 3m$		
c)	$27y - 5 = 16 - 1x$		

Bonus ▶

$342x - 158T + 140 - 3y = 2x + 356y - 52$		

A variable term has two parts: the variable and the coefficient.

the coefficient of *x* is −5

$-5x + 13$

the coefficient of *n* is +3

$27y + 3n - 5 = 16 - 1x$

8. Complete the table.

Expression	Variable Term	Variable	Coefficient	Constant Term
$-35x - 6$	$-35x$	x	-35	-6
$108 - 37M$				
$-23 + t$				
$1x$				

You can use variables, coefficients, and constant terms to represent real-world situations.

Use a variable for an unknown quantity, a coefficient with the variable for a quantity that changes as the variable changes, and a constant term for a quantity that does not change.

9. It costs $10 per hour to use a ski hill and $40 to rent skis.

a) Write an expression for the cost of renting skis and skiing for *h* hours. _____

b) What is the coefficient in your expression? _____

c) What is the constant term in your expression? _____

d) How much does it cost to rent skis and go skiing for 5 hours? _____

10. A truck is travelling at a speed of 50 km per hour.

a) Write an expression for the distance the truck travels in *h* hours. _____

b) What is the constant term? _____

c) What is the coefficient? _____

d) How far will the truck travel in 7 hours? _____

e) What does the variable in your expression represent? Circle the correct answer.

speed   number of hours   distance

11. A company charges a flat fee and an hourly rate to rent a scooter. Draw lines to match the coefficient, the constant term, and the variable with the correct quantities.

coefficient   the flat fee

constant term   the hourly rate

variable   the number of hours rented

PR7-11 Linear Relations in Four Quadrants

> REMINDER: The x-coordinate of a point is negative if the point is to the left of the y-axis.
> The y-coordinate of a point is negative if the point is below the x-axis.

1. a) Write the coordinates of the points.

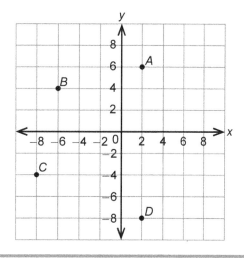

  A (　　,　　)　　B (　　,　　)

  C (　　,　　)　　D (　　,　　)

  b) Plot and label the points on the grid.

  E (−4, −8)　　　　　F (6, 3)

  G (6, −6)　　　　　H (−4, 6)

> The **y-intercept** is the value of y where a line crosses the y-axis.

2. a) Write the y-intercept of the line. Mark a point for the y-intercept on the grid.

i)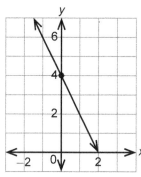

ii)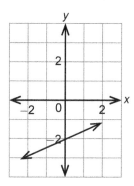

iii)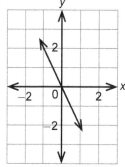

　　y-intercept: __4__　　　　　　y-intercept: _____　　　　　　y-intercept: _____

  b) Write the coordinates of the point you marked in part a) where the line crosses the y-axis.

  i) __(　,　)__　　　　ii) _____　　　　iii) _____

  c) Look at your answers to part b). What can you say about the x-coordinate of each point?
     What can you say about the y-coordinate of each point?

Bonus ▶

  a) A line crosses the y-axis at the point (0, −907). What is the y-intercept of the line? _____

  b) The y-intercept of a line is 437. Write the coordinates of the point where the line crosses

     the y-axis. _____

3. a) Complete the table of values for the linear relation.

$y = 3x - 2$

x	y
−1	
0	
1	
2	

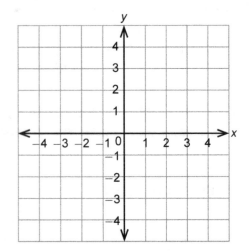

b) Graph the relation. Mark a point for the y-intercept.

c) Where does the y-intercept show up in the table?

The row where $x =$ _____. The y-intercept is _____.

All points on the y-axis have x-coordinate 0. To find the y-intercept of a linear relation using its formula, substitute 0 for x.

4. a) Substitute 0 for x to find the y-intercept of the linear relation.

i) $y = 13x - 5$
$y = 13(0) - 5$
$y = 0 - 5$
$y = -5$
y-intercept is −5

ii) $y = 27 - 15x$

iii) $y = -11 - 12x$

b) What is the constant term of the formula in part a)?

i) _____   **ii)** _____   **iii)** _____

c) How does the constant term compare to the y-intercept? _____

You can read the y-intercept and the change in y as x increases by 1 from the formula of a linear relation. Example:

coefficient (gap: change in y as x increases by 1) is −5

$y = -5 x + 3$

constant term (y-intercept) is +3

5. Write the y-intercept and the coefficient of x for the linear relation.

a) $y = 8x + 13$

y-intercept: _____

coefficient of x: _____

b) $y = -39x + (-28)$

y-intercept: _____

coefficient of x: _____

c) $y = -25x - 43$

y-intercept: _____

coefficient of x: _____

Bonus ▶ $-983 + 1 - x = y$

y-intercept: _____   coefficient of x: _____

6. Find the *y*-intercept and the gap between the *y*-values in the table. Then write a formula for the linear relation.

a)

x	y
−2	10
−1	6
0	2
1	−2

y-intercept: _____

gap: _____

formula: _y =_ _____

b)

x	y
−1	8
0	15
1	22
2	29

y-intercept: _____

gap: _____

formula: _____

c)

x	y
0	−1
1	−4
2	−7
3	−10

y-intercept: _____

gap: _____

formula: _____

7. Find the *y*-intercept and the coefficient of *x* (the change in *y* as *x* increases by 1) for the linear relation. Then write the formula.

a)

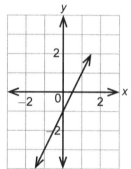

y-intercept: _____

coefficient of x: _____

formula: _y =_ _____

b)

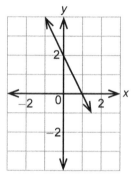

y-intercept: _____

coefficient of x: _____

formula: _____

c)

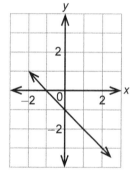

y-intercept: _____

coefficient of x: _____

formula: _____

8. Write the *y*-intercept and the coefficient of *x* (the change in *y* as *x* increases by 1) for the linear relation. Then sketch the graph.

$y = -2x + 3$

y-intercept: _____

coefficient of x: _____

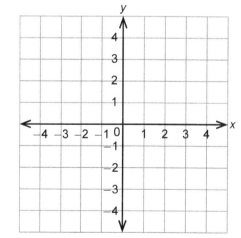

PR7-12 Solving Equations by Testing and Revising

A value for a variable that makes an equation true is called a **solution** to the equation.

Ezra writes an equation with one variable: $15x - 9 = 51$
He thinks that 4 might be the solution, so he substitutes it for x: $15(4) - 9$
Since $15(4) - 9 = 51$, the value 4 for x is the solution.

1. Use substitution to verify the solution to the equation.

   a) $25 + 14s = 53, s = 2$ b) $-40 + 3x = 50, x = 30$ c) $-18 - 5n + 4 = -1, n = 0$

   $LS = 25 + 14(2)$ $RS = 53$
   $\quad = 25 + 28$
   $\quad = 53$
   $LS = RS,$
   so $s = 2$ is the solution

2. Is the given value for the variable a solution to the equation? Check by substitution.

   a) $30y - 10 = 120, y = 4$ b) $-28 + b = -33, b = -5$ c) $42 - n = 5n + 10, n = 7$

   $LS = 30(4) - 10$ $RS = 120$
   $\quad = 120 - 10$
   $\quad = 110$
   $LS \neq RS,$
   so 4 is not the solution

   Bonus ▶ $7x - 300 + 4(8) = -690 + 20x + (54 \div 2), x = 30$

3. Marta and Raj worked on different math problems. Fill in the blanks with "Marta," "Raj," or "Marta and Raj."

   Marta: Raj:
   $5h + 21$ $5h + 21 = 61$
   when $h = 8$,   try $h = 8$
   $5(8) + 21$ $\quad LS = 5(8) + 21$ $RS = 61$
   $= 40 + 21$ $\quad\quad = 40 + 21$
   $= 61$ $\quad\quad = 61$
                          $\quad LS = RS,$ so $h = 8$ is the solution

   a) _____ used substitution.

   b) _____ tested a possible solution to an equation.

   c) _____ only evaluated an expression for a value of the variable.

   d) _____ simplified an expression after using substitution.

Solving an equation with one variable means finding the solution: the value for the variable that makes the equation true.

4. Solve for x by guessing and checking. Use the table.

a) $6x + 19 = 43$

x	$6x + 19$	True?
1		
2		
3		
4		
5		

so $x =$ _____

b) $20x - 35 = 65$

x	$20x - 35$	True?
1		
2		
3		
4		
5		

so $x =$ _____

c) $11x - 40 = -18$

x	$11x - 40$	True?
0		
1		
2		
3		
4		

so $x =$ _____

5. Substitute 5 for n and say whether 5 is too high or too low. Then try a higher or lower number.

a) $15 + 5n = 35$

n	$15 + 5n$	Answer
5	$15 + 5(5)$	40

5 is _____

b) $12n - 7 = 65$

n	$12n - 7$	Answer
5		

5 is _____

c) $8n + 37 = 93$

n	$8n + 37$	Answer
5		

5 is _____

d) $6n - 100 = -82$

n	$6n - 100$	Answer
5		

5 is _____

e) $6n + 100 = 136$

n	$6n + 100$	Answer
5		

5 is _____

f) $-80 + 10n = 0$

n	$-80 + 10n$	Answer
5		

5 is _____

6. Solve for x by guessing, checking, and revising. Use test values between 0 and 10.

a) $24x + 17 = 137$

b) $-18 + 7x = -4$

c) $13x - 19 = 98$

PR7-13 Solving One-Step Equations Using Models

1. The bag has an unknown number of apples. Let x represent the number of apples in the bag. Write an expression to represent the total number of apples.

   a) _____ b) _____ c) _____

2. The scales are balanced. Let m represent the number of apples in the bag. Write an equation to represent the total number of apples on each side of the balance.

   a) _____ b) _____

3. You start with balanced scales. If you perform the action, what action must you perform on the other side to maintain the balance?

   a) add 8 apples to the right side _____

   b) remove 5 apples from the left side _____

   c) subtract 13 apples from the right side _____

   d) add 20 apples to the left side _____

   Bonus ▶ remove a bag with n apples from the right side _____

4. In this model circles represent apples, a rectangle represents a bag with an unknown number of apples, and a line divides two sides of a balance. Write the equation represented by the model.

   a) _____ b) _____

5. a) Draw more circles so that the model represents the equation $x + 3 = 8$.

   b) Cross out circles from both sides of the model to get the bag by itself on one side. Write a new equation to show removing circles from both sides. _____

   c) Draw a final picture with the crossed-out circles removed. Write an equation to represent your final picture.

   _____

6. Each bag has the same unknown number of apples. Let y represent the number of apples in one bag. Write an expression to represent the total number of apples.

a)

_____3y_____

b)

_____

c)

_____

7. The scales are balanced. Let m represent the number of apples in one bag. Write an equation to represent the total number of apples on each side of the balance.

a)

_____

b)

_____

> An equation is like balanced scales. If you add, subtract, multiply, or divide on one side, you must do the same on the other side to preserve the balance, or equality.

8. If you perform the action on one side of an equation, what must you do on the other side to make sure the two sides are equal?

a) You multiply the left side by 5. _____

b) You divide the right side by 14. _____

9. In this model circles represent apples, rectangles represent bags with the same unknown number of apples, and the line divides two sides of a balance.

a) Add to the model to represent the equation $3m = 12$.

b) To get one bag by itself on one side, first show how to divide both sides of the model into equal groups. Write a new equation to show your division on both sides. _____

c) Draw a final picture after the division, showing just one of the equal groups on each side. Write an equation. _____

d) Verify your solution works by substituting the value for m into the equation from part a).

Patterns and Relations 7-13

PR7-14 Solving One-Step Equations Using Opposite Operations

1. Write the number that makes the equation true.

   a) $8 + 10 -$ _____ $= 8$

   b) $58 - 26 +$ _____ $= 58$

   c) $35 \times 20 \div$ _____ $= 35$

   Bonus ▶

   d) $n + 1 -$ _____ $= n$

   e) $250 + 306 -$ _____ $= 306$

   f) $987 + m -$ _____ $= m$

2. Write the operation that makes the equation true.

   a) $86 + 33 \bigcirc 33 = 86$

   b) $77 \div 7 \bigcirc 7 = 77$

   c) $h \times 333 \bigcirc 333 = h$

   d) $d - 274 \bigcirc 274 = d$

   e) $(45 \times p) \bigcirc 45 = p$

   f) $25x \bigcirc 25 = x$

3. Write the operation and number that make the equation true.

   a) $37 + 9$ _____ $= 37$

   b) $60 \div 15$ _____ $= 60$

   c) $38 - 75$ _____ $= 38$

   d) $m \times 7$ _____ $= m$

   e) $(9 \times g)$ _____ $= g$

   f) $10w$ _____ $= w$

   Bonus ▶ $(16 + 45x - 26y) \times 25$ _____ $= 16 + 45x - 26y$

4. The operation is applied to a starting number. How could you undo the operation and get back to the number you started with?

   a) add 24 __subtract 24__

   b) multiply by 7 _____

   c) subtract x _____

   d) divide by K _____

   e) add t _____

   f) multiply by n _____

To solve $x + 4 = 10$, subtract 4 from both sides of the equation.

$$x + 4 = 10$$
$$x + 4 - 4 = 10 - 4$$
$$x = 6$$

The variable x has been **isolated** since it is by itself on one side of the equation.

---

5. Isolate the variable by applying the same operation on both sides of the equation.
   Adjust the picture to show the first step. Then draw a new picture to isolate the variable.

   a) $s + 3 = 8$

   b) $3x = 6$

   $s + 3 - 3 = 8 - 3$

   _____ $=$ _____

   $3x \div 3 = 6 \div 3$

   _____ $=$ _____

Addition and subtraction are **opposite operations**, as are multiplication and division.
Even without a model, you can use opposite operations to isolate a variable in an equation.

6. Isolate the variable by applying the opposite operation. Remember to apply the same operation on both sides of the equation.

a) $17 + x = 35$

$17 + x - 17 = 35 - 17$
$x = 18$

b) $64 = 14 + x$

c) $z - 48 = 152$

d) $v \times 20 = 220$

e) $150 = 6b$

f) $r \div 25 = 13$

7. Check your solutions to Question 6 by substituting your solution into the original equation.

a) $LS = 17 + x$ $RS = 35$
$LS = 17 + 18$
$LS = 35$
$LS = RS,$
so $x = 18$ is the solution

b) $LS = 64$ $RS = 14 + x$

c) $LS =$

d)

e)

f)

REMINDER: Division is often written in fractional form.

Examples: $27 \div 9 = \dfrac{27}{9}$ $7 \div 10 = \dfrac{7}{10}$ $x \div 3 = \dfrac{x}{3}$ $19 \div w = \dfrac{19}{w}$

8. Solve for the variable by applying the opposite operation. Use fraction notation for division.

a) $7x = 91$

$\dfrac{7x}{7} = \dfrac{91}{7}$

$x = 13$

b) $14y = 42$

c) $50q = 450$

Sometimes the solution to an equation is a fraction or decimal number.

9. Solve for the variable by applying opposite operations to both sides of the equation. Use fraction notation for division. Leave the solution in fraction form.

a) $80w = 20$

$\dfrac{80w}{80} = \dfrac{20}{80}$

$w = \dfrac{20}{80} = \dfrac{1}{4}$

b) $26x = 13$

c) $9n = 7$

Patterns and Relations 7-14

PR7-15 Undoing Two or More Operations

1. Each bag contains the same unknown number of apples. Write the equation shown by the balanced scale. Use *b* for the unknown number of apples in a bag.

   a)

   _____ = _____

   b)

   _____

2. The circles represent apples, the rectangles represent bags with the same unknown number of apples, and the line divides two sides of a balance. Write the equation shown by the picture. Use *n* for the unknown number of apples in each bag.

   a)

   $2n + 3 = 9$

   b)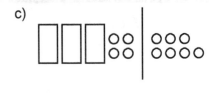

   _____

   c)

   _____

3. Draw a model to represent the equation.

   a) $2x + 5 = 11$

   b) $3x + 4 = 13$

   c) $13 = 4x + 5$

4. Solve the equation by using a model. Draw the new model and equation for each step of your solution.

   a) $2x + 3 = 7$

   $2x + 3 - 3 = 7 - 3$

   $2x = 4$

   $\dfrac{2x}{2} = \dfrac{4}{2}$

   $x = 2$

   b) $2x + 4 = 10$

5. Write the operations in words, in the correct order. Start with the variable.

a) $13 + 8p$
   Start with p. Multiply by 8. Add 13.

b) $(x - 35) \div 27$

6. Write an expression to match the description in words. Use brackets only when you need to.

a) Start with x. Multiply by 9. Then add 3.

b) Start with q. Divide by 15. Then subtract 12.

c) Start with w. Subtract 23.
   Then divide by 100.

Bonus ▶ Start with v. Divide by 14. Subtract 201.
Multiply by 49.

To undo two or more operations, undo the operations in reverse order. Example:

Start at 20. 20 20 Get back to 20.
Multiply by 3. 60 60 Divide by 3.
Add 7. 67 ⟶ 67 Subtract 7.

---

7. Do the operations and then undo them in reverse.

Start at 11. $\underline{\quad 11 \quad}$

Add 4. $\underline{\quad 15 \quad}$

Divide by 3. $\underline{\qquad\qquad}$

Subtract 1. $\underline{\qquad\qquad}$

Multiply by 6. $\underline{\qquad\qquad}$ *Divide by 6.*

8. Find the result. Then write the operations to get back to the starting number.

a) Start at 25. Multiply by 3. Add 12.
   $25 \times 3 + 12$
   $= 75 + 12$
   $= 87$ *Subtract 12. Divide by 3.*

b) Start at 46. Subtract 10. Divide by 3.

9. Write the result as an expression. Then write the operations to get back to the variable.

a) Start with x. Multiply by 4. Add 9.
   $4x + 9$
   Subtract 9. Divide by 4.

b) Start with m. Divide by 14. Subtract 20.

c) Start with r. Multiply by 4. Divide by 9.

d) Start with z. Multiply by 34. Subtract 85.

Bonus ▶ Start with y. Multiply by 14. Divide by 11. Add 23. Subtract 8.

PR7-16 Solving Equations with Two or More Operations

1. Aki performs operations starting with a secret number. Her result is 43. Write an equation and then work backwards to find the secret number.

   a) **Aki's operations**   **Work backwards to find n**

   | Start with n. | n | Write the equation again. | $4n - 5 = 43$ |

   Start with n. ___n___   Write the equation again. ___$4n - 5 = 43$___

   Multiply by 4. ___$4n$___   Undo subtracting 5 by adding 5. ___$4n - 5 + 5 = 43 + 5$___

   Subtract 5. ___$4n - 5$___   Write the new equation (simplify). ___$4n = 48$___

   The result is 43. ___$4n - 5 = 43$___   Undo multiplying by 4 by dividing by 4. ___$4n \div 4 = 48 \div 4$___

   Simplify. You solved for n! ___$n = 12$___

   Check your solution by doing the operations in order, the way Aki did them.

   Start with your solution: ___12___ Multiply by 4: ___48___ Subtract 5. ___43___ Did you get 43? ___yes___

   b) **Aki's operations**   **Work backwards to find q**

   Start with q. _____   Write the equation again. _____

   Divide by 5. _____   Undo adding 24 by subtracting 24. _____

   Add 24. _____   Write the new equation (simplify). _____

   The result is 43. _____   Undo dividing by 5 by multiplying by 5. _____

   Simplify. You solved for q! _____

   Check your solution by doing the operations in order, the way Aki did them.

   Start with your solution: _____ Divide by 5: _____ Add 24. _____ Did you get 43? _____

2. Solve the equation by applying opposite operations. Show each step.

   a) $11x - 10 = 78$

   $$11x - 10 + 10 = 78 + 10$$
   $$11x = 88$$
   $$11x \div 11 = 88 \div 11$$
   $$x = 8$$

   b) $30w + 11 = 221$

   c) $\dfrac{t}{6} + 38 = 47$

3. Check your solutions to Question 2 by substituting them into the original equations.

   a) $LS - 11(8) \quad 10 \quad RS - 78$ b)   c)

   $$= 88 - 10$$
   $$= 78$$
   $LS = RS,$
   so $x = 8$ is the solution

4. Solve the equation by applying opposite operations. Show each step.

a) $8x \div 12 = 6$

$8x \div 12 \times 12 = 6 \times 12$
$8x = 72$
$8x \div 8 = 72 \div 8$
$x = 9$

b) $\dfrac{10m}{7} = 30$

c) $\dfrac{7w}{2} = 49$

5. Check your solutions to Question 5 by substituting them into the original equations.

a) $LS = 8(9) \div 12 \quad RS = 6$

$=$

$=$

b)

c)

When solving an equation with two or more operations, isolate the variable by undoing the operations in reverse order.

Example: In the equation $\dfrac{5x}{6} + 9 = 19$, three things happen to x: multiply x by 5, divide by 6, and then add 9.

To isolate x, work backwards: subtract 9, multiply by 6, and then divide by 5 on both sides of the equation.

---

6. Solve the equation by applying opposite operations. Describe each step in words.

a) $\dfrac{5x}{6} + 9 = 19$

$\dfrac{5x}{6} + 9 - 9 = 19 - 9$ _subtract 9_

$\dfrac{5x}{6} = 10$ _simplify_

$\dfrac{5x}{6} \times 6 = 10 \times 6$ _multiply by 6_

$5x = 60$ _simplify_

$5x \div 5 = 60 \div 5$ _divide by 5_

$x = 12$ _simplify_

b) $\dfrac{10n}{14} - 4 = 1$

_____

_____

_____

_____

_____

_____

c) $3y \div 2 + 28 = 40$

d) $4n \div 5 - 13 = 7$

7. Nahid has 3 bags of apples and 2 extra apples. Each bag of apples has the same number of apples. In total, Nahid has 17 apples. Answer the questions to find out how many apples Nahid has in each bag.

a) Let b stand for the number of apples in each bag. Write an expression for the total number of apples inside the bags.

b) Write an expression using the variable b for the total number of apples Nahid has.

c) Use your expression from part b) and the total number of apples to write an equation.

d) Solve the equation for b by using a picture model. Use rectangles for bags with the unknown number of apples, and circles for apples. The first picture has been started for you. Write the equations that match each step of the solution.

_____

e) How many apples are in each of Nahid's bags? Write your answer as a complete sentence.

8. At an amusement park, admission costs $20 and each ride costs $3. Amo spent $95 in total.

a) How many rides did Amo go on? Write an equation to solve the problem. Show each step of your work. Write a concluding statement.

Bonus ▶ If Amo had gone on double the number of rides, how much would he have spent?

PR7-17 Solving Equations with Integers

1. Solve the equation by applying opposite operations. Show your work.

   a) $y + 9 = 3$
      $y + 9 - 9 = 3 - 9$
      $y = -6$

   b) $g - 23 = -11$

   c) $x + 39 = -86$

2. Check your solutions to Question 1 by substituting them into the original equations.

   a) $LS = (-6) + 9 \quad RS = 3$
      $LS = 3$
      $LS = RS,$
      so $y = -6$ is the solution

   b)

   c)

REMINDER: You can rewrite integer addition or subtraction without brackets.

Rules:	Examples:
$+ (+) = +$	$(-3) + (+7) = -3 + 7$
$+ (-) = -$	$(-3) + (-7) = -3 - 7$
$- (+) = -$	$(-3) - (+7) = -3 - 7$
$- (-) = +$	$(-3) - (-7) = -3 + 7$

---

3. Solve the equation. Show your work.

   a) $m + (-17) = -45$
      $m - 17 = -45$
      $m - 17 + 17 = -45 + 17$
      $m = -28$

   b) $p - (-25) = -55$

   c) $-3 + q + (+8) = -62 - (+2)$

   Bonus ▶ $(-75) + w - (-13) - (-12) = -200 - (+30) - (-40)$

4. Talia uses a model to solve the equation. The rectangle represents the variable x, white counters represent negative numbers, and black counters represent positive numbers. A pair of negative and positive counters on the same side cancel each other out. Write the equations that match each step of Talia's work.

   a) $x + (-4) = -2$

   $x + (-4) + (+4)$
   $= -2 + (+4)$

   $x + (\cancel{-4}) + (\cancel{+4})$
   $= +2$

   $x = +2$

   b) $x - (-2) = -1$

   $x + 2 = -1$

---

5. Solve the equation using pictures. Write an equation to match each picture in your solution. Remember, opposite integers add to 0 and cancel each other out.

a) $m - (-3) = -1$

$m + (+3) = -1$

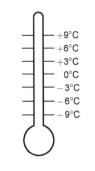

b) $n + (-2) = -3$

6. The coldest temperature on Thursday was −9 degrees Celsius. This was 4 degrees colder than Wednesday's coldest temperature.

a) Complete the statement: Let W be the _____.

b) Write an expression with W for the coldest temperature on Wednesday. Hint: Since Thursday is colder than Wednesday, do you need to add or subtract?

_____

c) Use your expression from part b) and the actual coldest temperature on Thursday

to write an equation. _____

d) Solve your equation from part c) using pictures. Write equations to match each picture.

e) What was the coldest temperature on Wednesday? Write your answer as a complete sentence.

7. Cleopatra was born before the common era (BCE). Julius Caesar died 25 years after Cleopatra was born, in the year 44 BCE. Answer the questions to find out when Cleopatra was born.

a) Complete the statement: Let x stand for _____.

b) Write and solve an equation using the variable x. Show each step of your work.

c) In what year was Cleopatra born? Write a concluding statement.

Bonus ▶ Three biologists are climbing a ladder out of an underground bat cave. Salma is 25 metres below Ross, while Jin is 34 metres above Ross. Jin is at an altitude of −35 metres. At what altitude is Salma? Use an equation to solve the problem. Show each step of your work.

PR7-18 Problems and Puzzles: Equations

To solve word problems, it can be helpful to translate words into mathematical expressions. Key words give clues about the operations needed. Examples:

Add	Subtract	Multiply	Divide
increased by	decreased by	double	divided by
sum	difference	product	quotient
more than	less than	twice as many	divided into
total	reduced by	times	shared equally

1. Match the description with the correct algebraic expression.

   a) 2 more than a number $4x$ b) 2 divided into a number $3n$

        a number divided by 3 $x - 2$ a number reduced by 4 $n \div 2$

        2 less than a number $x + 2$ a number times 3 $n + 3$

        the product of a number and 4 $x - 3$ twice as many as a number $n - 4$

        a number decreased by 3 $x \div 3$ a number increased by 3 $2n$

2. Write an algebraic expression for the description.

   a) four more than a number   _____   b) a number decreased by 10   _____

   c) the product of 7 and a number   _____   d) the sum of a number and 7   _____

   e) a number divided by 8   _____   f) two less than a number   _____

   g) five times a number   _____   h) 6 divided into a number   _____

When solving word problems, the word "is" means "equal" and it translates to the equal sign, $=$.

Example: "Two more than a number is seven" can be written as $x + 2 = 7$.

3. Translate the sentence into an equation.

   a) Four more than a number is eighteen.

   $x + 4 = 18$

   b) Five less than a number is twelve.

   c) Five times a number is thirty.

   d) Six divided into a number is four.

   e) A number multiplied by 2 then increased by 5 is 35.

   f) A number multiplied by three then decreased by four is seventeen.

   g) 3 times a number is 4 less than 28.

   Bonus ▶ Two more than half of a number is five more than three.

4. Translate the sentence into an equation. Solve the equation to find the number.

    a) A number multiplied by 3 then increased by 7 is 31.

    b) A number multiplied by four then decreased by twenty is forty-four.

Bonus ▶

    c) 5 more than 4 times a number is 6 less than the product of 13 and 3.

    d) Seven more than a number divided by twenty is two less than the product of three and six.

5. Keegan goes on a road trip with his uncle. They drive at a speed of 80 km per hour. They makes two stops, the first for 20 minutes and the second for 40 minutes. The trip takes a total of 7 hours. What distance do they travel?

6. Ava is 4 times as old as her son. Ava's younger brother is 39. The difference between Ava's and her brother's age is 5 years. How old is Ava's son?

Bonus ▶ Ed's sister is 3 years younger than Ed. Ed's mother is 3 times Ed's age. Ed's father is 4 years older than Ed's mother. The sum of all four ages is 89. How old is Ed's mother?

SS7-12 Area of Parallelograms

1. Move the shaded triangle to make a rectangle with the same area as the parallelogram. Find the base and the height of the parallelogram and the width and the height of the rectangle.

a)

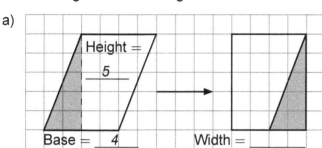

Height = _____

b)

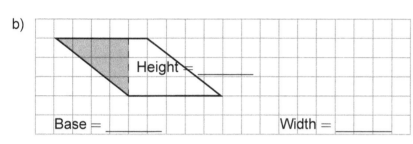

Height = _____

2. Convert the parallelogram into a rectangle with the same area. Find the base and the height of the parallelogram and the width and the height of the rectangle.

a)

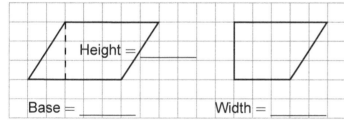

Height = _____

b)

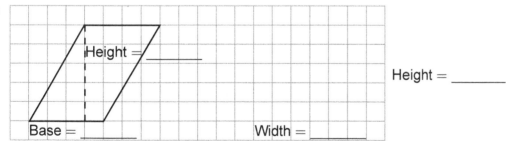

Height = _____

3. a) Look at your answers for Questions 1 and 2. Complete each sentence with the word "base" or "height."

The height of the rectangle is the same as the _____ of the parallelogram.

The width of the rectangle is thew same as the _____ of the parallelogram.

b) Area of rectangle = width × height. What is the formula for the area of a parallelogram?

Area of parallelogram = _____ × _____

Area of parallelogram = base × height	or	$A = b \times h$

4. Find the area of the parallelogram given the base and height.

a) Base = 5 cm

Height = 7 cm

Area = _____

b) Base = 4 m

Height = 3 m

Area = _____

c) Base = 8 mm

Height = 6.5 mm

Area = _____

d) Base = 3.7 cm

Height = 6 cm

Area = _____

Any side of a parallelogram can be used as a base. The height is always perpendicular to the base.

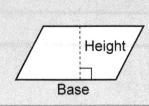 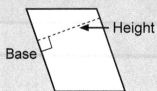 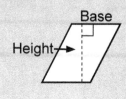

5. Find the area in two ways, by using different sides as the base. Use a millimetre ruler.

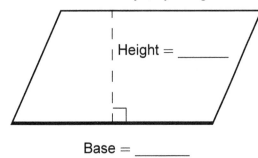

Height = _____

Base = _____

Area = _____

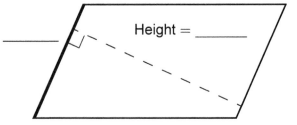

Base = _____

Height = _____

Area = _____

6. Draw a perpendicular to the base of the parallelogram (the thick line) using a set square.

Measure the base and the height of the triangle to the closest tenth of a centimetre. Calculate the area.

a)

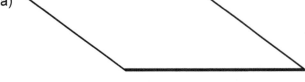

b)

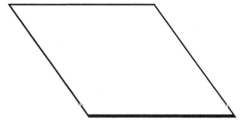

 7. A bus has ten windows that are parallelograms with height 1 m and base 1.3 m. Glass costs $23 for each 1 m². How much will it cost to replace the glass in all ten windows?

SS7-13 Area of Triangles

Two identical right triangles can be arranged to make a rectangle.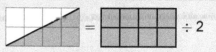
Area of right triangle = Area of rectangle ÷ 2

1. Find the area of the triangle in square units.

a)

Area = _____

b)

Area = _____

c)

Area = _____

d)

Area = _____

2. Draw a line to divide the triangle into two right triangles. Find the areas of all the triangles in square units.

a)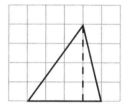

Triangle 1 = ___6___

Triangle 2 = ___2___

Total area = ___8___

b)

Triangle 1 = _____

Triangle 2 = _____

Total area = _____

c)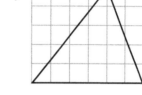

Triangle 1 = _____

Triangle 2 = _____

Total area = _____

d)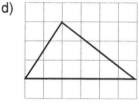

Triangle 1 = _____

Triangle 2 = _____

Total area = _____

3. Rectangle C is made of Rectangles A and B. Triangle C is made of Triangles A and B.

a) Find the areas.

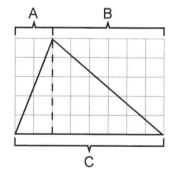

Area of Rectangle A = _____   Area of Triangle A = _____

Area of Rectangle B = _____   Area of Triangle B = _____

Area of Rectangle C = _____   Area of Triangle C = _____

b) What fraction of the area of Rectangle C is the area of Triangle C?

4. Jun says, "The area of Triangle T is half of the area of the rectangle."

Is he correct? Explain. _____

_____

_____

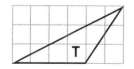

Triangles have **base** and **height**. Height is measured along a perpendicular from a vertex to the base.

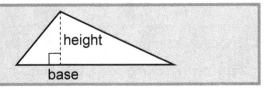

5. a) Each grid square is 1 cm². Draw a rectangle around the triangle. Then fill in the table.

	i)	ii)	iii)
Base of Triangle	5 cm		
Height of Triangle	4 cm		
Width of Rectangle	5 cm		
Height of Rectangle	4 cm		
Area of Rectangle	20 cm²		
Area of Triangle	10 cm²		

   b) Look at the table in part a). Complete each sentence with the word "base" or "height."

   The height of the rectangle is the same as the _____ of the triangle.

   The width of the rectangle is the same as the _____ of the triangle.

Area of triangle = (base × height) ÷ 2   or $A = (b \times h) \div 2$

6. Find the area of the triangle given the base and height. Do not forget the units.

   a) Base = 5 cm   b) Base = 4 cm   c) Base = 8 cm   d) Base = 3.7 cm

   Height = 8 cm   Height = 3 cm   Height = 6 cm   Height = 6 cm

   Area = _____   Area = _____   Area = _____   Area = _____

7. Find the area of the triangle.

   a)   b)   c)   d)

   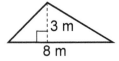   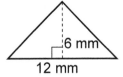   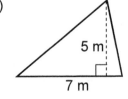   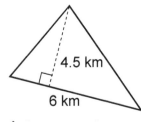

   Area = _____   Area = _____   Area = _____   Area = _____

SS7-14 Area of Triangles and Parallelograms

1. The base is shown by a thick line. Label the height of the parallelogram with *h*.

a) 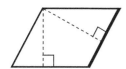   b) 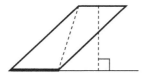   c)    d)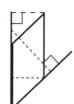

Bonus ▶ Find the area of the parallelogram.

a) 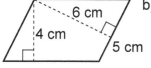   b) 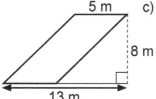   c) 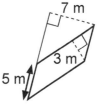   d)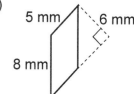

2. Draw a rectangle around the triangle. Then find the area of each triangle.

a) 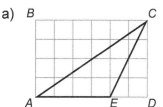   b) 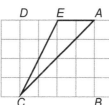   c)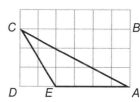

Area of triangle *ACD* _____	Area of triangle *ACD* _____	Area of triangle *ACD* _____
Area of triangle *ECD* _____	Area of triangle *ECD* _____	Area of triangle *ECD* _____
Area of triangle *AEC* _____	Area of triangle *AEC* _____	Area of triangle *AEC* _____

3. Measure the base and height of the triangle. Then find the area of the triangle.

a)    b) 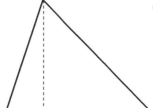   c)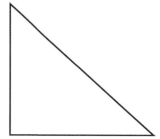

Base = _____	Base = _____	Base = _____
Height = _____	Height = _____	Height = _____
Area = _____	Area = _____	Area = _____

4. Find the area of the triangle with the given dimensions.

a) Base = 6 cm

   Height = 2 cm

   Area = _____

b) Base = 4 m

   Height = 6 m

   Area = _____

c) Base = 6 mm

   Height = 3.6 mm

   Area = _____

d) Base = 3.2 cm

   Height = 8 cm

   Area = _____

5. In the triangle, the thick line is the base. Use a set square or a protractor to draw the height. Then measure the base and the height and fill in the table.

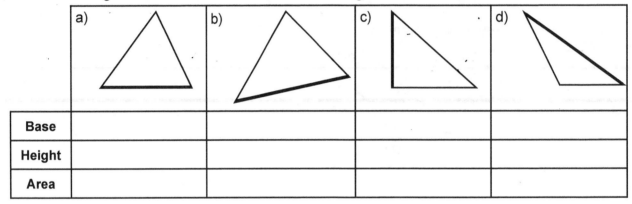

	a)	b)	c)	d)
Base				
Height				
Area				

6. a) A plot of land is a triangle with a base of 37 m and a height of 40 m. What is its area?

   b) A park is a right triangle with a base of 2 km and a height of 1.5 km. What is its area?

   c) A company's logo is a triangle with a base of 12.5 cm and a height of 6 cm. What is its area?

7. Find the area of the triangle.

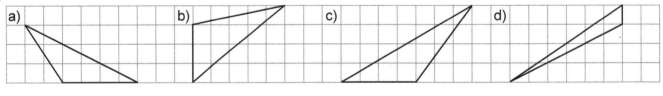

Bonus ▶ e)

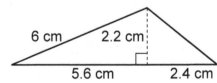

f)

5.7 cm   2.5 cm
2.6 cm   2.5 cm

6 cm   2.2 cm
5.6 cm   2.4 cm

8. a) Find the base, height, and area of each triangle. What do you notice?

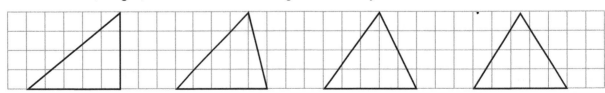

   b) On grid paper, draw two different triangles with the same base and height. What do you know about their areas?

SS7-15 Working with Area Problems

1. a) Fill in the supplied measurements. Use a variable for what you do not know.

	Problem	Base or Width	Height	Area
i)	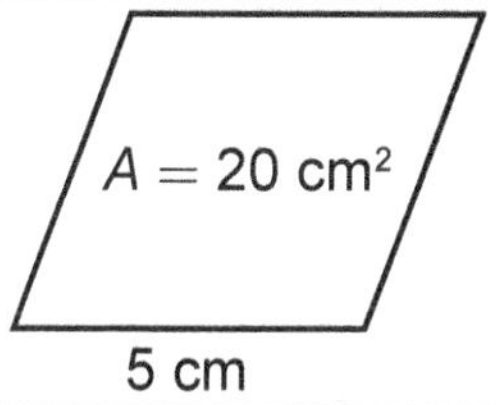 $A = 20$ cm^2 5 cm	5 cm	h	20 cm^2
ii)	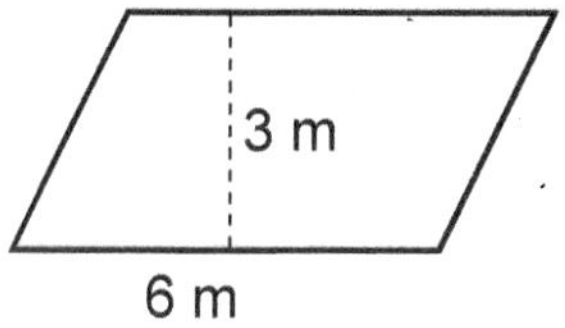 3 m 6 m			
iii)	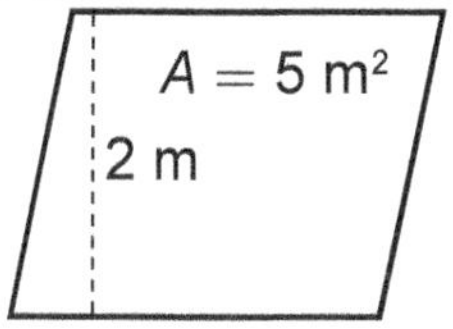 $A = 5$ m^2 2 m			
iv)	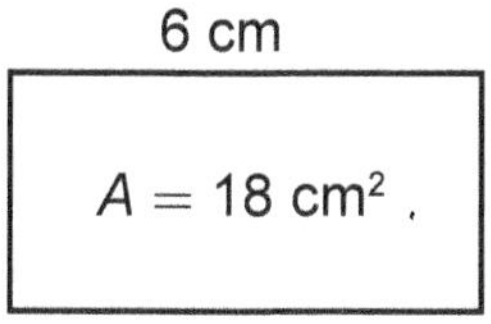 6 cm $A = 18$ cm^2			
v)	A rectangle with area 24 cm^2 has height 3 cm. What is its width?			
vi)	A triangle has base 43 mm and height 36 mm. What is its area?			
vii)	A parallelogram with base 4 km has area 20 km^2. What is the height of the parallelogram?			
viii)	A rectangle has width 7 m and height 6 m. What is its area?			

b) For each problem in the table in part a), use the area formula to write an equation. Then solve the equation for the variable.

i) $5\,cm \times h = 20\,cm^2$ ii)   iii)   iv)

   $h = 20\,cm^2 \div 5\,cm$

   $= 4\,cm$

v)   vi)   vii)   viii)

2. Organize the data. Write the formula you could use and an equation. Then solve the equation to find the unknown measurement.

a) A parallelogram has base 5 cm and area 35 cm². What is its height?

Given: _____base = 5 cm_____   Equation: ___5 cm × h = 35 cm²___

_____area = 35 cm²_____   5h = 35

Find: _height of parallelogram_   h = 35 ÷ 5

Formula: _Area = base × height_   = 7 cm

b) What is the height of a parallelogram with base 3 m and area 12 m²?

Given: _____   Equation: _____

_____

Find: _____

Formula: _____

c) A triangle has an area of 300 cm² and height of 10 cm. What is the length of its base?

Given: _____   Equation: _____

_____

Find: _____

Formula: _____

d) A vegetable garden is a rectangle that covers 2.4 m². It is 3 m long. How wide is it?

Given: _____   Equation: _____

_____

Find: _____

Formula: _____

e) On a sign outside a store, there is a company logo that is a parallelogram with a height of 80 cm. It covers an area of 6000 cm². How long is the horizontal side of the logo?

80 cm

f) A triangular flowerbed has an area of 10.2 m². The longest side of the triangle is 6 m long. How far from the longest side is the opposite corner of the flowerbed?

8 cm

Bonus ▶ A hexagon with sides of 8 cm each and a total area of 168 cm² is made of three identical rhombuses. What is the area of each rhombus? What is the height of each rhombus?

8 cm
?

3. A parallelogram has a base of 2 m and a height of 80 cm.

   a) Lynn thinks its area is $2 \times 80 = 160$ cm². Is she correct? Explain.

   b) Cam thinks its area is $2 \times 80 = 160$ m². Is he correct? Explain.

   c) 80 cm = 0.8 m
      Find the area of the parallelogram in metres squared (m²).

   d) Convert the base of the parallelogram to centimetres. Then find the area of the parallelogram in centimetres squared (cm²).

   e) Is your area in part c) equal to your area in part d)? If not, find your mistake.

4. A triangular water fountain in a mall has an area of 3.25 m². Its shortest side is 125 cm long. What is the distance from the shortest side to the opposite corner of the water fountain?

5. Find the area of the shaded shape.

   a)

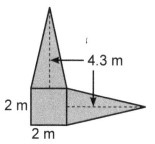

   b)

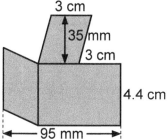

   c)

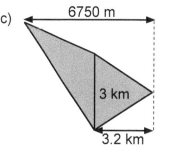

6. A rectangular lawn has a path in it in the shape of a parallelogram. The shaded areas are grass.

   a) What is the height of the parallelogram that makes the path?

   b) The path, measured along the side of the rectangle, is 140 cm wide. What is the area of the path?

   c) What is the total area covered in grass? Show your work.

   d) The path is covered in gravel. It costs $3 per square metre. The soil for the lawn costs $8.50 per square metre, and the grass sod costs $3.50 per square metre. How much do the materials for the lawn cost in total?

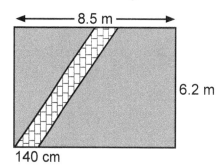

7. The shape at right is made from two parallelograms. Its area is 32.5 m². What is the height of the larger parallelogram?

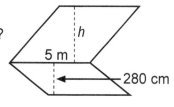

Bonus ▶The ancient Maya used units of length called kaans. A particular ancient Mayan field was rhombus shaped. Its area was 20 square kaans. Each side of the field was 5 kaans long. What was the distance between the opposite sides of the field?

SS7-16 Radii and Diameters of Circles

All points on a circle are the same distance from the **centre** of the circle.

To construct a circle with centre O and passing through point P, use a compass.

Step 1: Put the point of the compass at the centre of the circle.

Step 2: Put the pencil of the compass at point P.

Step 3: Keeping the point at the centre, and without changing the distance from the compass point to the pencil point, draw the circle.

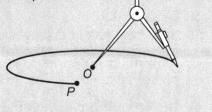

1. Draw a circle with centre O that passes through point P.

   a)

   O•   P•

   b)

   P•

   O•

   c)

   O•

   P•

The **radius** of a circle is the distance of any point on the circle from the centre.

To construct a circle with centre O and a radius of 3 cm, use a compass.

Step 1: Set the distance from the compass point to the pencil point to 3 cm.

Step 2: Put the point of the compass on the centre of the circle. Keep the width the same!

Step 3: Draw the circle.

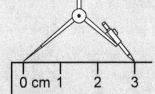

2. Draw a circle with centre O and the given radius r.

   a) $r = 2$ cm   b) $r = 15$ mm   c) $r = 25$ mm

   •O   •O   •O

A **diameter** of a circle is any line segment that passes through the centre of the circle and joins two points on the circle. The lengths of all the diameters of a circle are all the same and are also called the diameter (d). The diameter is:

• the largest width across the circle.

• always double the radius (r), so $d = 2 \times r$.

3. Which is given, the radius or the diameter? Find the measurement that is not given.

a)

$r =$ _____ mm

$d =$ _____ mm

b)

$r =$ _____ mm

$d =$ _____ mm

c)

$r =$ _____ mm

$d =$ _____ mm

4. Draw a line through the centre of the circle. Measure the radius and diameter.

a)

$r =$ _____ mm

$d =$ _____ mm

b)

$r =$ _____ mm

$d =$ _____ mm

c)

$r =$ _____ mm

$d =$ _____ mm

5. Use a ruler to find the point on the circle farthest from the given point. Then draw the diameter through those two points and find its length.

a)

Diameter = _____ mm

b)

Diameter = _____ mm

c)

Diameter = _____ mm

6. a) For each circle in Question 5, draw another diameter. Measure the length of the new diameter. If you do not get the same length both times, find your mistake.

b) How can you tell where the centre of the circle is?

7. Construct three circles with the same centre and diameters of 70 mm, 5 cm, and 2.4 cm.

SS7-17 Pi and Circumference

The distance around a polygon is called its **perimeter**.

The distance around a circle is called its **circumference**.

INVESTIGATION ▶ What is the quotient of the circumference and diameter of a circle?

A. Calculate the quotient of circumference (C) ÷ diameter (d). Round your answer to two decimal places.

a) C = 16.34 cm

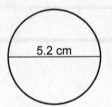

5.2 cm

C ÷ d = _____

b) C = 25.13 m

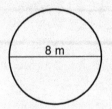

8 m

C ÷ d = _____

c) C = 56.55 mm

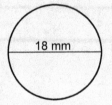

18 mm

C ÷ d = _____

d) C = 8 cm

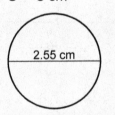

2.55 cm

C ÷ d = _____

e) C = 13 m

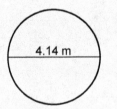

4.14 m

C ÷ d = _____

Bonus ▶ C = 94.25 km

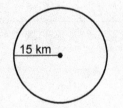

15 km

C ÷ d = _____

B. What do you notice about your answers to Part A? _____

_____

The quotient of C ÷ d is the same for all circles. Mathematicians give the quotient a special name:

$$\pi = C \div d$$

The symbol π is pronounced "pie." The number π has an infinite number of digits after the decimal point. To six decimal places,

$$\pi \approx 3.141593$$

---

1. Round π to the given decimal place.

a) π ≈ _____ (tenths)

b) π ≈ _____ (hundredths)

c) π ≈ _____ (thousandths)

d) π ≈ _____ (ten thousandths)

If you know the diameter (*d*) of a circle, you can find the circumference (*C*).

$$C = \pi \times d \text{ (or } C = \pi d)$$

You can use 3.14 for π to get a good approximation.

Example: If $d = 4$ cm, then use $C = \pi \times 4$ cm ≈ 12.57 cm.

So, $C ≈ 12.57$ cm

2. Find the circumference of the circle with the given diameter. Include the units in your answer.

a)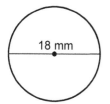
18 mm

b)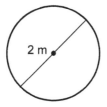
2 m

c)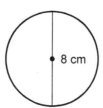
8 cm

d)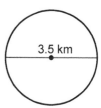
3.5 km

$C ≈$ _3.14 × 18 mm_ $C ≈$ _____ $C ≈$ _____ $C ≈$ _____

$C ≈$ _56.52 mm_ $C ≈$ _____ $C ≈$ _____ $C ≈$ _____

If you know the radius of a circle, you can find the circumference:

$$C = \pi \times d$$
$$= \pi \times 2 \times r$$
$$= 2\pi r$$

---

3. Find the circumference of the circle with the given radius. Include the units. Use 3.14 for π.

a)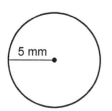
5 mm

b)
6 m

c)
9 km

d)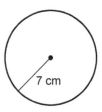
7 cm

$C ≈$ _____ $C ≈$ _____ $C ≈$ _____ $C ≈$ _____

$C ≈$ _____ $C ≈$ _____ $C ≈$ _____ $C ≈$ _____

4. Find the circumference. Include the units.

a)
14 cm

b)
6 m

c)
7 cm

d)
11 km

5. Which two parts of Question 4 have the same answer? Why is this the case?

SS7-18 Estimating Area of Circles

1. Estimate the area of the circle by finding the area of the shaded parts.

   a) Find the area of each shaded shape in the top right quarter of the circle.

   b) Add the areas in part a) to estimate the area of one quarter of the circle. _____

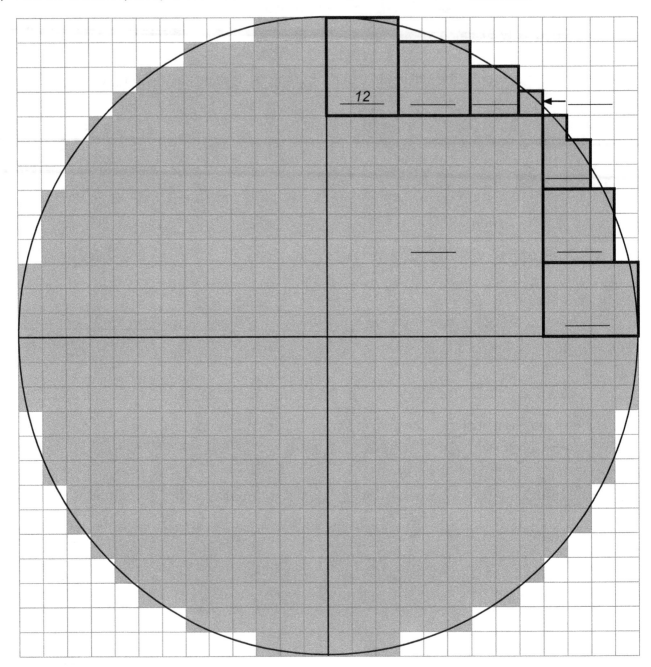

   c) Find the area of the entire shaded part of the grid using your answer from part b). $A =$ _____

   d) The radius of the circle is $r =$ _____.

   e) Use a calculator to calculate $A \div (r \times r)$ to two decimal places.

      What does the answer tell you? _____

   f) Explain why the area A that you found in part c) is a good estimate for the area of the circle.

Shape and Space 7-18

SS7-19 Area of Circles

1. Dov cut a circle into 12 parts and rearranged them.

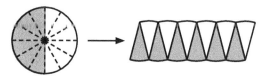

a) What distance does the arrow show? Write "radius," "diameter," "circumference," or "half the circumference."

   i)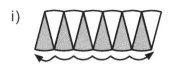

   _____

   ii)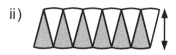

   _____

b) Dov drew a parallelogram around the pieces of the circle. Use your answers from part a) to make the sentence true.

   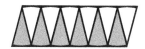

   i) The base of the parallelogram is close to _____ of the circle.

   ii) The height of the parallelogram is close to _____ of the circle.

c) Explain why half of the circumference is $\pi \times r$. _____

   _____

d) The area of the parallelogram is close to the area of the circle. Use your answers in parts b) and c) to write a formula for the area of a circle.

   $A =$ _____

2. Find the area of the circle with the given radius.

   a)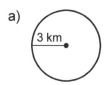

   3 km

   $A \approx$ _____

   $A \approx$ _____

   b)

   8 cm

   $A \approx$ _____

   $A \approx$ _____

   c)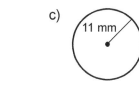

   11 mm

   $A \approx$ _____

   $A \approx$ _____

   d)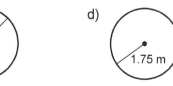

   1.75 m

   $A \approx$ _____

   $A \approx$ _____

3. Find the radius of the circle. Then find the area.

   a)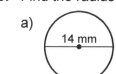

   14 mm

   $r =$ __7 mm__

   $A \approx$ __3.14 × 7 × 7__

   $A \approx$ __153.86 mm²__

   b)

   10 m

   $r =$ _____

   $A \approx$ _____

   $A \approx$ _____

   c)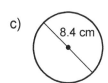

   8.4 cm

   $r =$ _____

   $A \approx$ _____

   $A \approx$ _____

   d)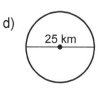

   25 km

   $r =$ _____

   $A \approx$ _____

   $A \approx$ _____

SS7-20 Problems Related to Circles

1. What fraction of the circle is shaded?

a)

$$\frac{90°}{360°} = \frac{1}{4}$$

b)
240°

c)

d)
45°

2. A circle has an area of 36 cm². Find the area of the shaded part.

a)

$A = \frac{1}{2} \times 36$

$A = \underline{\ 18\ cm^2\ }$

b)

$A =$

$A = \underline{\hspace{2cm}}$

c)
120°

$A =$

$A = \underline{\hspace{2cm}}$

d)
120°

$A =$

$A = \underline{\hspace{2cm}}$

3. A **sector** is a part of a circle that is bound by two radii and a part of the circumference.
   Find the area of the sector.

a)
11 m   11 m

b)
8.8 km

c)
5.1 cm   135°

Bonus ▶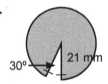
30°   21 mm

4. What fraction of the circumference is thick? Write your answer in lowest terms.

a)

$$\frac{90°}{360°} = \frac{1}{4}$$

b)

c)
120°

d)

5. Each circle in Question 4 has a diameter of 20 cm. Find the length of the thick part of the circle.

a)   b)   c)   d)

6. Find the distance (D) around the shape.

a)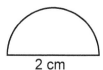

2 cm

Curved side: $\pi \times d \div 2$

$\approx 3.14 \times 2\ cm \div 2$

$= 3.14\ cm$

$D \approx 3.14\ cm + 2\ cm$

$= 5.14\ cm$

b)

3 m

c)

5 m

d)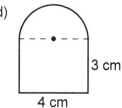

3 cm

4 cm

7. Find the radius of the circle given its circumference C.

a) $C = 314$ cm   b) $C = 157$ m   c) $C = 69.08$ m   **Bonus** ▶ $C = 75.4$ cm

$C = 2\pi \times r$

$314 \approx 2 \times 3.14 \times r$

$314 \approx 6.28 \times r$

$r \approx 314 \div 6.28 = 50$

8. Find the areas of the circles in Question 7.

9. Two circles, A and B, are drawn on 1-cm grid paper.

a) How many times as large as the radius of A is the radius of B?

b) How many times as large as the circumference of A is the circumference of B?

c) How many times as large as the area of A is the area of B?

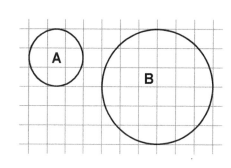

SS7-21 Problems and Puzzles: Area and Circumference

REMINDER: 1 km = 1000 m   1 m = 100 cm   1 cm = 10 mm

3.54 km = 3.54 × 1000 m = 3540 m   27 mm = 27 ÷ 10 cm = 2.7 cm

Use a calculator for all problems in this lesson.

1. Find the area of the shape made of triangles, rectangles, or parallelograms.

a)

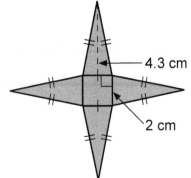

4.3 cm

2 cm

b)

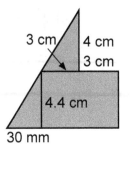

3 cm   4 cm

3 cm

4.4 cm

30 mm

c)

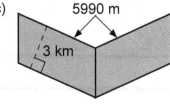

5990 m

3 km

2. A garden has a path in the shape of a parallelogram. The shaded areas are flower beds.

a) Find the area of the path and of the flower beds.

b) The path will be covered in tiles which cost $30 per square metre. Plants for the flower bed will cost about $25 per square metre. What is the cost of materials for the garden?

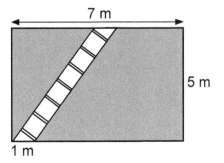

7 m

5 m

1 m

In all questions that follow, round your answer to two decimal places.

3. The shape is made of triangles, parallelograms, and halves or quarters of circles. Find the area and the distance around the shape.

a)

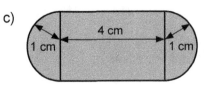

72 mm

4 cm

6 cm

b)

282 cm   282 cm

2 m   2 m   2 m

c)

4 cm

1 cm   1 cm

4. A tractor wheel has a diameter of 1 m. About how many times would the wheel turn if the tractor drove 100 m?

5. a) Find the area of each shaded part and unshaded part. Use 3.14 for π.

i)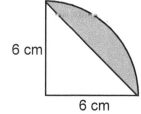
6 cm

6 cm

ii)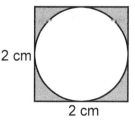
2 cm

2 cm

iii)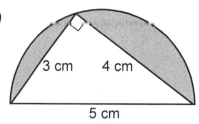
3 cm   4 cm

5 cm

b) Look at the pictures in part a). Is the area of the shaded part more or less than the area of the unshaded part? Do your answers for part a) make sense with the pictures? Explain.

6. A window has the shape of a rectangle with a semicircle on top. The width of the rectangle and the diameter of the circle are both 90 cm. The height of the rectangle is 1.4 m. If glass costs $25 per 1 m², what is the cost of the glass needed to build the window?

7. A lawn in front of a library is getting redone. It will have a path that follows the arc of a quarter circle, as shown.

a) What is the area of the path?

b) The grey quarter circle will be groundcover. The path will be tiled. The rest of the area will be a grass lawn. The groundcover costs $6 per square metre, tiles cost $9 per square metre, and the grass for the lawn costs $5.50 per square metre. How much will the project cost?

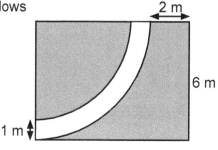
2 m

6 m

1 m

8. The London Eye is a giant Ferris wheel in downtown London, England.

a) The diameter of the wheel is about 135 m. What is the circumference of the wheel?

b) The wheel turns about 0.3 m every second. About how long does it take for the wheel to rotate once?

c) The London Eye has 32 evenly spaced capsules that can each hold 25 people.

  i) How many people can ride the Ferris wheel at the same time?

  ii) How far apart are the capsules?

d) La Grand roue de Montréal is the largest Ferris wheel in Canada. Its 42 cabins each hold 8 people and are about 4.5 m apart.

  i) How many people can ride La Grand roue at one time?

  ii) Which is taller: La Grand roue or the London Eye? By how much? How do you know?

1. Use long division to write the fraction as a decimal. Keep dividing until the division ends.

a) $\dfrac{2}{5} =$ _____

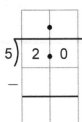

b) $\dfrac{1}{4} =$ _____

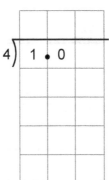

c) $\dfrac{3}{8} =$ _____

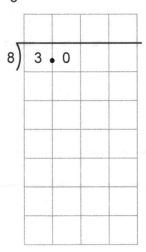

2. a) Calculate $2 \div 3$ by writing 2 as 2.0, 2.00, and 2.000.

$2.0 \div 3$

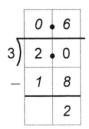

$2.00 \div 3$

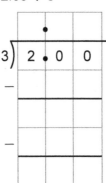

$2.000 \div 3$

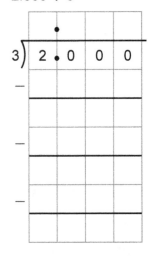

b) What patterns do you see in part a)?

c) Predict $2.0000 \div 3$. Do you need to start the division from the beginning again?

3. Use long division to write the fraction as a decimal. Stop adding zeros to the dividend when the division ends, or when you see a pattern.

a) $\dfrac{1}{9} =$ ___0.111...___

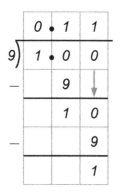

b) $\dfrac{3}{4} =$ _____

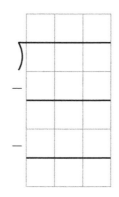

c) $\dfrac{8}{9} =$ _____

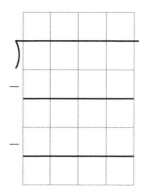

In a **repeating decimal** a digit or group of digits repeats forever. The part that repeats is called the **repeating core**. In bar notation, the repeating core is indicated with a bar over it.

Examples: $0.55555.... = 0.\overline{5}$ $4.12121212... = 4.\overline{12}$ $7.0161616... = 7.0\overline{16}$

A **terminating decimal** does not go on forever. Examples: 5.68, 0.444, 2.75

---

4. Circle the repeating decimals.

   0.12345   0.22222...   0.77   0.512512512...   0.0252525...

5. Extend the decimal to fill in all the blanks.

a) $0.3 \approx 0.3$ ___ ___ ___ ___

b) $0.203 \approx 0.203$ ___ ___ ___ ___

c) $0.52 \approx 0.$ ___ ___ ___ ___

d) $0.817 \approx 1.$ ___ ___ ___ ___ ___ ___

Bonus ▶ $8.2539 \approx 8.$ ___ ___ ___ ___ ___ ___ ___ ___

6. Write the repeating decimal using bar notation.

a) $0.88... =$ ___$0.\overline{8}$___

b) $0.3434... =$ _____

c) $57.1222... =$ _____

d) $8.45757... =$ _____

e) $17.031212... =$ _____

f) $0.036713671... =$ _____

REMINDER: In a decimal fraction, the denominator is a power of ten.

   Example: $\dfrac{3}{100}$ is a decimal fraction. $\dfrac{3}{100} = 0.03$

---

7. Write the decimal fraction as a decimal.

a) $\dfrac{3}{10} =$ _____

b) $\dfrac{87}{100} =$ _____

c) $\dfrac{429}{1000} =$ _____

8. a) Use long division to write the fraction as a decimal. Stop adding zeros to the dividend when the division ends or when you see a pattern. Use bar notation for repeating decimals.

i) $\dfrac{4}{5}$ = _____

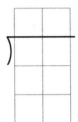

ii) $\dfrac{2}{9}$ = _____

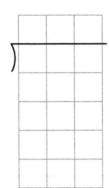

iii) $\dfrac{7}{9}$ = _____

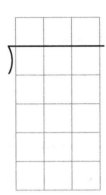

b) Which fraction in part a) can be written as a terminating decimal? _____

c) Which decimals in part a) are repeating decimals? _____

The denominator of some fractions can be written as products of 2s, 5s, or both.

Examples: $\dfrac{7}{10} = \dfrac{7}{2 \times 5}$ $\dfrac{7}{8} = \dfrac{7}{2 \times 2 \times 2}$ $\dfrac{92}{125} = \dfrac{92}{5 \times 5 \times 5}$

---

9. Write the denominator as a product of 2s, 5s, or both.

a) $\dfrac{8}{25}$ = _____

b) $\dfrac{27}{50}$ = _____

c) $\dfrac{99}{100}$ = _____

To decide if a fraction can be written as a terminating or repeating decimal:

Step 1: Write the fraction in lowest terms.

Step 2: Look at the denominator. If it can be written as a product of only 2s, 5s, or both, the decimal terminates. If it cannot be written as a product of only 2s, 5s, or both, the decimal repeats.

---

10. a) Write the fraction in lowest terms, then write the denominator as a product of 2s, 5s, or both, if possible.

i) $\dfrac{12}{40}$ = _____ = _____

ii) $\dfrac{35}{60}$ = _____ = _____

iii) $\dfrac{44}{80}$ = _____ = _____

b) Can the denominator in part a) be written as a product of only 2s, 5s, or both?

i) _____   ii) _____   iii) _____

c) Can the fraction in part a) be written as a terminating decimal?

i) _____   ii) _____   iii) _____

---

11. Predict whether the decimal will terminate. Use a calculator to check your answers.

a) $\dfrac{7}{8}$
   b) $\dfrac{3}{4}$
   c) $\dfrac{56}{80}$
   d) $\dfrac{63}{77}$
   e) $\dfrac{25}{55}$

12. Are the decimal equivalents for $\dfrac{1}{3}$, $\dfrac{2}{9}$, and $\dfrac{18}{27}$ repeating or terminating decimals?

How can you tell without calculating the decimal?

13. a) Write the sixths from $\dfrac{1}{6}$ to $\dfrac{5}{6}$ in lowest terms.

b) Predict which of the sixths will terminate. Explain.

c) Use long division to calculate the decimal equivalents for each of the sixths.

d) Which of the sixths terminate? Was your prediction in part b) correct? If not, find your mistake.

14. The denominators of $\dfrac{3}{6}$, $\dfrac{3}{12}$, $\dfrac{6}{12}$, $\dfrac{9}{15}$ and $\dfrac{12}{15}$ all have 3 as a factor, but their decimal equivalents are not repeating decimals.

a) How can you tell that they are terminating decimals?

b) Use long division to confirm that fractions terminate. Reduce each fraction to lowest terms before dividing.

$\dfrac{3}{6} = \dfrac{1}{2}$
$\dfrac{3}{12} = \underline{\quad}$
$\dfrac{6}{12} = \underline{\quad}$
$\dfrac{9}{15} = \underline{\quad}$
$\dfrac{12}{15} = \underline{\quad}$

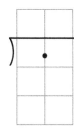
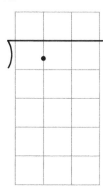
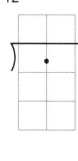
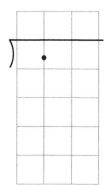
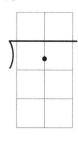

Number 7-39

1. Write the decimal as a decimal fraction.

   a) $0.5 = \dfrac{5}{10}$

   b) $0.74 =$

   c) $0.826 =$

   d) $0.4531 =$

2. Write "terminating" or "repeating."

   a) A fraction in lowest terms has denominator 99. Its decimal representation is _____.

   b) A fraction in lowest terms has denominator 100. Its decimal representation is _____.

3. a) Write the fraction as a decimal using bar notation.

   i) $\dfrac{1}{9} = \underline{0.\overline{1}}$

   ii) $\dfrac{7}{9} = \underline{\quad\quad}$

   iii) $\dfrac{5}{9} = \underline{\quad\quad}$

   iv) $\dfrac{3}{9} = \underline{\quad\quad}$

   v) $\dfrac{4}{9} = \underline{\quad\quad}$

   vi) $\dfrac{6}{9} = \underline{\quad\quad}$

   vii) $\dfrac{8}{9} = \underline{\quad\quad}$

   viii) $\dfrac{2}{9} = \underline{\quad\quad}$

   b) Describe the pattern in the decimals in part a).

4. a) Write the fraction as a decimal using bar notation.

   i) $\dfrac{27}{99} = \underline{\quad\quad\quad}$

   ii) $\dfrac{83}{99} = \underline{\quad\quad\quad}$

   iii) $\dfrac{20}{99} = \underline{\quad\quad\quad}$

   iv) $\dfrac{64}{99} = \underline{\quad\quad\quad}$

   v) $\dfrac{98}{99} = \underline{\quad\quad\quad}$

   vi) $\dfrac{15}{99} = \underline{\quad\quad\quad}$

   b) Describe the pattern in the decimals in part a).

5. Extend the patterns in your answers for Questions 3 and 4 to write the fraction as a decimal. Check your answer with a calculator.

   a) $\dfrac{414}{999} = \underline{\quad\quad\quad}$

   b) $\dfrac{3572}{9999} = \underline{\quad\quad\quad}$

   c) $\dfrac{2}{99} = \underline{\quad\quad\quad}$

   d) $\dfrac{2}{999} = \underline{\quad\quad\quad}$

   e) $\dfrac{67}{999} = \underline{\quad\quad\quad}$

   Bonus ▶ $\dfrac{4143}{99\,999} = \underline{\quad\quad\quad}$

6. Describe what happens when you write a fraction with a denominator of 9, 99, 999, and so on, as a decimal.

7. a) Was the fraction converted into a repeating decimal correctly? If yes, write "correct." If not, write "incorrect" and the correct decimal.

i) $\dfrac{89}{99} = 0.9898...$ _____*incorrect—it should be 0.8989...*_____

ii) $\dfrac{9}{99} = 0.0909...$ _____

iii) $\dfrac{8010}{9999} = 0.08100810...$ _____

iv) $\dfrac{40}{99} = 0.4040...$ _____

v) $\dfrac{1}{11} = 0.0909...$ _____

vi) $\dfrac{10}{11} = 0.9090...$ _____

vii) $\dfrac{9}{999} = 0.00090009...$ _____

viii) $\dfrac{677}{9999} = 0.677677...$ _____

Bonus ▶ $\dfrac{32\,323\,232}{99\,999\,999} = 0.3232...$ _____

b) What do you notice about parts ii) and v)? Explain.

8. Write the repeating decimal as a fraction.

a) 0.008008...

b) 0.2121...

c) 0.0606...

d) 0.04150415...

e) 0.30043004...

f) 72.7272...

g) 893.08930893...

h) 1.00010001...

Bonus ▶ 4 760 221.47602214760221...

Nick has 6 muffins. He wants to give $\frac{2}{3}$ of his muffins to his friends.

To do so, he shares the muffins equally using 3 plates:

There are 3 equal groups, so each group is $\frac{1}{3}$ of 6.

There are 2 muffins in each group, so $\frac{1}{3}$ of 6 is 2.

There are 4 muffins in two groups, so $\frac{2}{3}$ of 6 is 4.

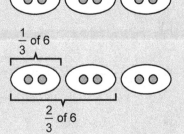

1. Use the picture to find the fraction of the number.

a)

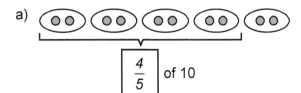

$\boxed{\dfrac{4}{5}}$ of 10

b)

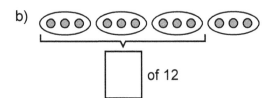

$\boxed{}$ of 12

2. Fill in the missing numbers.

a)

$\boxed{\dfrac{1}{3}}$ of 9 = ___3___

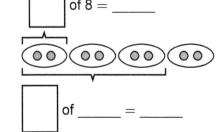

$\boxed{\dfrac{2}{3}}$ of ____ = ____

b)

$\boxed{}$ of 8 = ____

$\boxed{}$ of ____ = ____

c)

$\boxed{}$ of 12 = ____

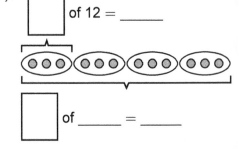

$\boxed{}$ of ____ = ____

d)

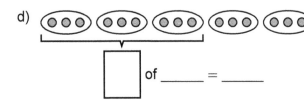

$\boxed{}$ of ____ = ____

e)

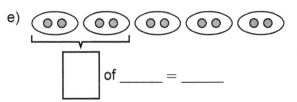

$\boxed{}$ of ____ = ____

3. Circle the given amount.

a) $\frac{2}{3}$ of 9

b) $\frac{4}{5}$ of 10

c) $\frac{3}{4}$ of 8

d) $\frac{2}{5}$ of 15

4. Draw the correct number of dots in each group. Then circle the given amount.

a) $\frac{2}{3}$ of 12

b) $\frac{2}{3}$ of 15

5. Find the fraction of the whole amount by sharing the food equally. Hint: Draw the correct number of plates and place the items one at a time. Then circle the correct amount.

a) Find $\frac{1}{4}$ of 20 rotis.

$\frac{1}{4}$ of 20 is _____

b) Find $\frac{1}{2}$ of 10 kebabs.

$\frac{1}{2}$ of 10 is _____

c) Find $\frac{2}{3}$ of 9 spring rolls.

$\frac{2}{3}$ of 9 is _____

d) Find $\frac{4}{4}$ of 12 churros.

$\frac{4}{4}$ of 12 is _____

Kate finds $\frac{2}{3}$ of 15 as follows:

Step 1: She finds $\frac{1}{3}$ of 15 by dividing 15 by 3.

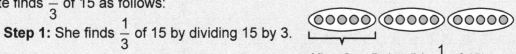

$15 \div 3 = 5$ (so 5 is $\frac{1}{3}$ of 15)

Step 2: Then she multiplies the result by 2.

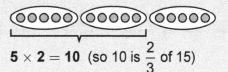

$5 \times 2 = 10$ (so 10 is $\frac{2}{3}$ of 15)

6. Find the amount using Kate's method.

a) $\frac{3}{5}$ of 10 = ___6___

$10 \div 5 = 2, 3 \times 2 = 6$

b) $\frac{2}{6}$ of 18 = _____

c) $\frac{2}{7}$ of 28 = _____

d) $\frac{3}{9}$ of 18 = _____

e) $\frac{5}{8}$ of 24 = _____

f) $\frac{2}{5}$ of 35 = _____

7. Explain why Question 6 parts b) and d) have the same answer.

8. Braden gave away three quarters of his 20 trading cards. How many trading cards does he still have? _____

A fraction compares a part to a whole. A **ratio** can compare a part to a part, or a part to a whole.

Example: ◯◯☐☐◯

The **part-to-part ratio** of circles to squares is 3 to 2 or 3 : 2.

The **part-to-whole ratio** of circles to shapes is 3 to 5 or 3 : 5.

1. ☆ ◖ ◯ ☐ ◯ ◯ ◯ ☐ ☆ △ ◯ ☆ ◯ ◖ ☐

   a) The ratio of stars to moons is __3__ : __2__.   b) The ratio of triangles to moons is _____ : _____.

   c) The ratio of squares to circles is _____ : _____.   d) The ratio of triangles to shapes is _____ : _____.

   Bonus ▶ The ratio of all shapes to shapes with exactly one line of symmetry is _____ : _____.

2. Yvette's fruit salad recipe calls for 4 cups of apples, 2 cups of oranges, and 3 cups of bananas.

   a) How many cups of fruit does Yvette need in total? _____

   b) What is the ratio of cups of oranges to cups of fruit salad? _____ : _____

3. A string of letters: **A E E U A E A U A A A**

   a) What does the ratio 3 : 2 describe in the letters above?

   b) What does the ratio 6 : 11 describe in the letters above?

4. The ratio of the circumference of any circle to its diameter is always π : 1, or approximately
   3.14 : 1. In other words, a circle whose diameter is 1 has a circumference of pi. This is true
   for any units. 3.14 cm : 1 cm, 3.14 m to 1 m, 3.14 km : 1 km. Fill in the missing information below.

Circumference : Diameter
3.14 : 1
_____ : 2
9.42 : _____
_____ : 4

Circumference : Diameter
π : 1
2π : _____
___π : 3
_____ : 4

5. Find the circumference of a circle with diameter 18. Represent the answer two ways:
   using just numbers, and using π.

In the picture, there are 3 circles for every 2 squares.

There are also 6 circles for every 4 squares.

The ratios 3 : 2 and 6 : 4 are **equivalent**.

6. Find two equivalent ratios for the picture.

a)

circles to squares = 1 : _____ = 2 : _____

b)

circles to squares = 2 : _____ = 6 : _____

7. Complete the pictures so the ratio of triangles to squares is the same in each column.
Then create a sequence of equivalent ratios.

Triangles	△ △	△ △ △ △	
Squares	☐ ☐ ☐		☐ ☐ ☐ ☐ ☐ ☐ ☐ ☐ ☐
Ratio	2 : 3		

8. Multiply both terms by the same numbers to write three equivalent ratios.

a) 2 : 3 = ___4___ : ___6___ = ___8___ : ___12___

b) 2 : 9 = _____ : _____ = _____ : _____

c) 7 : 4 = _____ : _____ = _____ : _____

d) 111 : 5 = _____ : _____ = _____ : _____

9. Find the missing terms.

a) 3 : 7 = _____ : 14

b) 5 : 6 = 10 : _____ = _____ : _____ 18

c) 2 : 5 = _____ : 50 = _____ : 5000

Bonus ▶ 4 : 3 = 32 : _____ = _____ : 300

A jar contains 5 blue marbles for every 2 red marbles. There are 15 blue marbles.

To find how many red marbles are in the jar, write a sequence of equivalent ratios.
Stop when there are 15 blue marbles.

The jar holds 6 red marbles.

Total number of marbles in the jar: 15 blue + 6 red = 21 marbles.

Blue		Red
5	:	2
10	:	4
15	:	6

10. A recipe for green paint says to mix 2 cups of blue paint with every 7 cups of yellow paint.

a) How much blue paint is needed to mix with 21 cups of yellow paint? _____

Bonus ▶ If the ratio of paint was reversed, and was 2 yellow : 7 blue, would that change
what the resulting green paint looked like? Explain.

A **percentage** is a ratio that compares a number to 100.

Percent means "for every 100" or "out of 100." For example, 84% on a test means 84 marks out of a possible 100 marks.

You can think of a percentage as a decimal fraction with denominator 100.

It has an equivalent decimal representation. Example: $45\% = \dfrac{45}{100} = 0.45$

1. Write the percentage as a fraction and a decimal.

   a) $7\% = \boxed{} = $ _____

   b) $92\% = \boxed{} = $ _____

   c) $50\% = \boxed{} = $ _____

2. Write the fraction as a percentage and a decimal.

   a) $\dfrac{31}{100} = $ _____ $= $ _____

   b) $\dfrac{100}{100} = $ _____ $= $ _____

   c) $\dfrac{1}{100} = $ _____ $= $ _____

3. Write the fraction as a percentage and a decimal by first changing it to a fraction with denominator 100. You may have to reduce the fraction first.

   a) $\dfrac{3 \times 20}{5 \times 20} = \dfrac{60}{100} = 60\%$

   b) $\dfrac{24}{30}$

   c) $\dfrac{17}{25}$

   d) $\dfrac{49}{70}$

If you use a thousands cube to represent 1 whole, you can see that taking $\dfrac{1}{10}$ of a number is the same as dividing the number by 10—the decimal point shifts one place left.

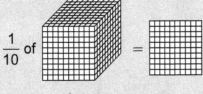

$\dfrac{1}{10}$ of = $\dfrac{1}{10}$ of = $\dfrac{1}{10}$ of = □

$\dfrac{1}{10}$ of $1 = 0.1$ $\dfrac{1}{10}$ of $0.1 = 0.01$ $\dfrac{1}{10}$ of $0.01 = 0.001$

4. Find $\dfrac{1}{10}$ of the number by shifting the decimal point. Write your answer in the box.

   a) 4   b) 9   c) 23   d) 210   e) 8.3   f) 5.2

   $\boxed{0.4}$ $\boxed{}$ $\boxed{}$ $\boxed{}$ $\boxed{}$ $\boxed{}$

5. 10% is equivalent to $\frac{10}{100}$ or $\frac{1}{10}$. Find 10% of the number.

a) 0   b) 7.5   c) 3.06   d) 6.45   e) 0.09   f) 12.2

You can easily find percentages of any number when the percentage is a multiple of 10.

Example: To find 30% of 21, find 10% of 21 and then multiply the result by 3.

Step 1: 10% of 21 = 2.1

Step 2: 3 × 2.1 = 6.3 ⟶ 30% of 21 = 6.3

---

6. Find the percentage using the method above.

a) 60% of 15

10% of _15_ = ☐

_6_ × ☐ = _____

b) 80% of 25

10% of _____ = ☐

_____ × ☐ = _____

c) 30% of 1.3

10% of _____ = ☐

_____ × ☐ = _____

To find 35% of 27, Marta follows these steps.

Step 1: She multiplies 27 by 35.

	2	3	
		2	7
×		3	5
	1	3	5
	8	1	0
	9	4	5

Step 2: She divides the result by 100.

945 ÷ 100 = 9.45

So 35% of 27 is 9.45.

---

7. Find the percentage using Marta's method.

a) 25% of 44 _____

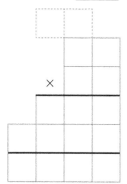

b) 18% of 92 _____

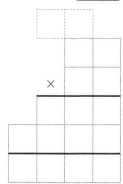

Amy says 35% can also be written as 0.35. To find 35% of 27, she multiplies 0.35 × 27.

8. Use Amy's method to find the percentage of the number.

a) 23% of 47 = _____ × _____ = _____

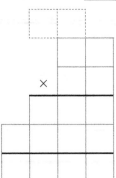

b) 92% of 49 = _____ × _____ = _____

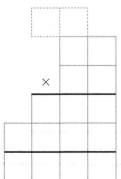

9. Find the percentage using Marta's method.

a) 23% of 23 _____

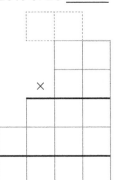

b) 15% of 26 _____

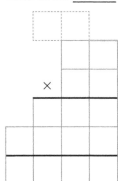

c) 64% of 58 _____

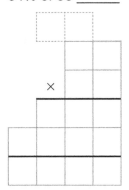

10. Find the percentage using Amy's method.

a) 23% of 23 _____

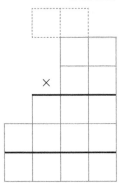

b) 15% of 26 _____

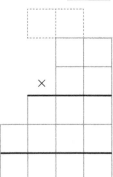

c) 64% of 58 _____

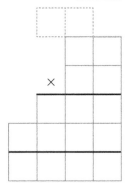

11. a) Should your answers to Questions 9 and 10 be the same or different? _____

b) If your answers to Questions 9 and 10 were not the same find and correct your mistake(s).

N7-44 Mental Math, Estimating, and Percentages

1. Mikael's meal cost $22.35. There is a 10% tax. Estimate how much money Mikael should leave in total if he wants to leave a tip of between 10% and 20%. Explain why you used this method to estimate.

2. Students categorized their favourite movies by continent or country of origin. Change the fraction to a percentage. Then find the percentage of movies in the third category.

   a) Brigitte's favourite movies

USA	Europe	Other
40%	$\frac{1}{2}$	$\frac{1}{10}$
= 40%	= 50%	= 10%

   b) Sandeep's favourite movies

Canada	India	Other
30%	$\frac{5}{10}$	

   c) Gabriel's favourite movies

Canada	South America	Other
$\frac{1}{2}$	40%	

3. Calculate the percentages mentally. Then add them.

   a) 20% of 40 is _____ and 80% of 40 is _____, so 20% of 40 + 80% of 40 is _____.

   b) 20% of 32 is _____ and 80% of 32 is _____, so 20% of 32 + 80% of 32 is _____.

   c) 40% of 300 is _____ and 60% of 300 is _____, so 40% of 300 + 60% of 300 is _____.

   d) 30% of 12 is _____ and 70% of 12 is _____, so 30% of 12 + 70% of 12 is _____.

4. Is 100% of each number in Question 3 equal to the number? _____ If not, find your mistake.

5. Vicky wants to save $\frac{1}{4}$ of her earnings and spend the rest. If she earns $120 a month, how much can she spend each month? Hint: First convert the fraction to a percentage.

6. Jim wants to pay for his $24 meal. He decides to round the price up to $30 instead of down to $20. Explain why he might choose to round up instead of down.

7. a) Find 35% of 40 in two ways. Show your work. Do you get the same answer both ways?

b) 35% is less than 50% or $\frac{1}{2}$. Is your answer to part a) less than half of 40? _____

c) Is 35% closer to 0 or to $\frac{1}{2}$? _____

d) Was your answer to part a) closer to 0 or to half of 40?

e) Is your answer to part a) reasonable? Explain.

8. a) Use Question 7 as a model for finding 75% of 80 in two ways. Do you get the same answer both ways? You are not limited to using the same methods used in Question 7.

b) 75% is greater than 50% or $\frac{1}{2}$. Is your answer to part a) greater than half of 80?

c) Is 75% closer to 50% or to 100%, or equally close to both?

d) Is your answer to part a) reasonable? Explain.

N7-45 Fractional Percentages

A **fractional percentage** is a ratio that compares a fraction to 100.

Percent means "for every 100" or "out of 100." For example, 84.5% on a test means 84.5 marks out of a possible 100 marks.

A fractional percentage has an equivalent decimal representation.

Example: $45\frac{1}{2}\% = 45.5\%$

1. Show the percentage on the grid.

   a) $4\frac{1}{2}\%$
   b) $23\frac{1}{2}\%$
   c) $60\frac{1}{2}\%$
   d) $49\frac{1}{2}\%$

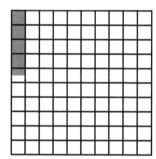 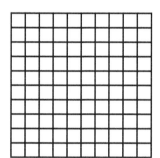 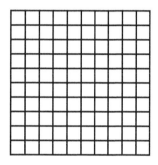 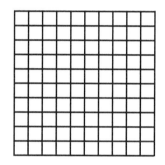

2. Convert the fractional percentage to a decimal percentage.

   a) $\frac{1}{4}\% = \frac{25}{100}\% = 0.25\%$
   b) $\frac{3}{5}\%$

   c) $\frac{17}{20}\%$
   d) $\frac{12}{16}\%$

3. Convert the fractional percentage to a decimal percentage.

   a) $16\frac{1}{4}\% = 16.25\%$
   b) $91\frac{3}{5}\%$
   c) $8\frac{17}{20}\%$
   d) $104\frac{12}{16}\%$

4. What power of ten should you multiply the decimal by to make it a whole number?

   a) 6.2 _____
   b) 19.88 _____
   c) 53.03 _____
   d) 71.245 _____

   e) 86.057 _____
   f) 33.006 _____
   Bonus ▶ 153.03231 _____

5. Write the percentage as a proper fraction.

   a) 7.4%
   b) 9.9 %
   c) 26.28%
   d) 75.031%
   Bonus ▶ 5609.0074%

   $= \dfrac{7.4}{100}$

   $= \dfrac{74}{1000}$

6. If a percentage has four digits after the decimal point, how many zeros will be in the denominator of its equivalent fraction? Explain.

7. Write the percentage as a decimal.

a) 9.4%   b) 9.2%   c) 19.8%   d) 65.75%   **Bonus ▶** 44.2819%

   $= 0.094$

8. If a percentage has five digits after the decimal point, how many digits after the decimal point will its equivalent decimal representation have? Explain.

9. Find 1% of the number.

a) 3   b) 28   c) 161   d) 9647   **Bonus ▶** 2 341 905 814

10. Use your answers to Question 9 to find 0.5% of the number. Show your work.

a) $0.5 \times 0.03 = 0.015$ b)   c)

d)   **Bonus ▶**

11. Find the percentage of the number. Show your work.

a) 0.35% of 7   b) 0.42% of 56   c) 0.03% of 109

   $0.35 \times (1\% \text{ of } 7)$

   $= 0.35 \times 0.07$

   $= 0.0245$

12. You know that 1% of a number is 16. Find the percentage of the number.

a) 0.3%   b) 0.9%   c) 0.62%

   $0.3 \times 16 = 4.8$

13. Express the percentage as the sum of a whole number and a decimal.

a) 35.3%   b) 108.03%   c) 467.49

   $= 35\% + 0.3\%$

14. Find the given percentage of the number by expressing the percentage as a sum of a whole number and a decimal and multiplying. Use a calculator to multiply.

a) 6.1% of 850   b) 9.8% of 50   c) 87.2% of 2350

   $6\% \text{ of } 850 + 0.1\% \text{ of } 850$

   $= 6 \times 8.5 + 0.1 \times 8.50$

   $=$

   $=$

You can add and subtract percentages just as you add and subtract whole numbers, decimals, and fractions.

Example: $10 + 5 = 15$, $\dfrac{10}{100} + \dfrac{5}{100} = \dfrac{15}{100}$, $10\% + 5\% = 15\%$

1. Add or subtract the percentages.

a) $20\% + 5\% =$ _____

b) $30\% + 20\% =$ _____

c) $10\% + 10\% =$ _____

d) $20\% - 5\% =$ _____

e) $50\% - 20\% =$ _____

f) $75\% - 10\% =$ _____

To find 5% of a number, first find 10% of the number. Then divide by 2.

To find 20% of a number, first find 10% of the number. Then multiply by 2.

2. Complete the table. Start by finding 10% of each number.

	60	300	30	40	70	90
5%	3		$\dfrac{3}{2} = 1.5$			
10%	6	30	3			
20%	12					
15% = 10% + 5%	9					

3. Mike wants to leave a 15% tip on a meal that cost $32 before tax. How much tip should he leave? Hint: Find 10% and then 5%.

4. Dylan wants to buy a $128 bike. There are two kinds of tax on it. One is a 7% tax and the other is an 8% tax.

a) Since the total tax is 15%, does he have to calculate 7% and 8% separately, or can he calculate it another way? Explain.

b) Calculate how much Dylan will pay in tax.

5. Carmel wants to know how much tax she has to pay on items from a hardware store.
A furnace filter and lightbulbs total $37.43. A battery costs $2.57.

a) Does Carmel need to calculate 5% of $37.43 and 5% of $2.57 separately or is there a simpler way? Explain.

b) How much is the tax?

When you pay 6% sales tax, you pay 100% of the price plus 6% of the price = 100% + 6%.

When you tip 11%, you pay 100% of the price plus 11% of the price = 100% + 11%.

When you pay 6% sales tax and a tip of 11% on the same purchase, you pay 100% of the price plus 6% of the price plus 11% of the price = 100% + 6% + 11%

6. a) You buy a baseball. The sales tax is 7%. The total = _____ % + _____ %.

b) You get a haircut. You leave a 12% tip. The total = _____ % + _____ %.

c) You dine out. The tax is 8%. You leave a tip of 13%. The total = _____ % + _____ % + _____ %.

7. The sales tax is 10%. Find the total cost for the item plus tax.

a) scooter: $108

tax = $___10.80___

total = $___118.80___

b) coat: $82

tax = $_____

total = $_____

c) book: $10

tax = $_____

total = $_____

8. The price of Ron's meal at a restaurant is $18 before taxes. The tax is 15%. Ron wants to leave a tip of 20% of the cost of the meal before taxes. How much will Ron pay in total?

9. A store charges 80¢ for each can of juice. The tax is 5%.

a) How much does each can cost including tax?

b) What is the cost of two cans, including tax?

10. Find the discount in dollars. Then find the sale price.

a) replacement bicycle chain: $32.99, with a 7% discount

b) new board game: $46.95, with a 13% discount

To encourage sales, stores often pay their salespeople a commission—a percentage of the price of the item that was sold.

1. A salesperson receives a 5% commission for each sale. Fill in the table.

Item	Unit Price	Quantity	Commission
hair clip	$1.20	1	*$0.06*
house	$500 000	1	
sweater	$50	1	
sweater	$50	11	
jacket	$165	1	
jacket	$165	4	

2. A painter spends $500.00 on supplies. Complete the table.

	Fraction of Money Spent	Percentage of Money Spent	Amount of Money Spent
Brushes			$50.00
Paint	$\dfrac{4}{10}$		
Canvas		50%	

3. a) Ivan spent 1 hour doing housework. The table shows the time (in minutes) spent on each chore. Complete the chart.

Chore	Fraction of 1 Hour	Percentage of 1 Hour	Decimal	Number of Minutes (Percentage × 60)
Laundry	$\dfrac{1}{4}$			$25 \times 60 \div 100 = 15$
Garbage	$\dfrac{1}{20}$	5%		
Vacuuming		50%		
Dishes			0.20	

b) How did you find the time spent doing 25 dishes?

4. For an art project, students created 16 photographs, 12 drawings, and 12 paintings. 25% of the photographs, 75% of the drawings, and 50% of the paintings show people. How many of the art projects do not show people?

5. Last year, Delia paid $200 every month for groceries. This year the cost of groceries has increased by 5%. Delia's salary also increased 5% this year.

a) How much did Delia spend on groceries last year?

b) How much will Delia spend on groceries this year?

c) If Delia's salary last year was $40 000, how much will it be this year?

d) What percentage of Delia's salary was spent on groceries last year?

e) What percentage of Delia's salary will be spent on groceries this year?

f) Your answers to parts e) and f) should be the same. Explain why that is.

1. A company charges a flat fee and an hourly rate to rent a bike. Draw lines to match the coefficient, the constant term, and the variable with the correct quantities.

   coefficient   the flat fee

   constant term   the hourly rate

   variable   the number of hours rented

2. Is the given value for the variable a solution to the equation? Check by substitution.

   a) $30y - 10 = 120$, $y = 4$ b) $-32 + b = -37$, $b = -5$ c) $53 - n = 5n + 21$, $n = 7$

   $LS = 30(4) - 10$ $RS = 120$

   $\quad = 120 - 10$

   $\quad = 110$

   $LS \neq RS$,
   so 4 is not a solution

   Bonus ▶ $12x - 288 + 6(7) = -678 + 32x + (70 \div 2)$, $x = 20$

3. Solve the equation by applying opposite operations. Show each step.

   a) $11x - 10 = 78$ b) $9w + 300 = 354$ c) $\dfrac{t}{6} + 67 = 76$

   $11x - 10 + 10 = 78 + 10$

   $\qquad 11x = 88$

   $11x \div 11 = 88 \div 11$

   $\qquad x = 8$

4. Marcella and Amo live in a city with transit. To ride a bus, they each need to buy a monthly transit card for $20 and pay $3 for each bus ride. Marcella buys a card and rides the bus for a month, spending a total of $98.

   a) How many bus rides does Marcella take during the month? Write an equation to solve the problem. Show each step of your work.

   b) Amo takes twice as many bus rides as Marcella. How much does Amo spend during the month?

5. A bus has ten windows that are parallelograms with height 1 m and base 1.3 m. Glass costs $26 for each 1 m². How much will it cost to replace the glass in all ten windows?

6. Construct two circles with the same centre. One with a radius of 5 cm and another with a diameter of 6 cm.

7. Find the area of and the distance around the shape.

a)

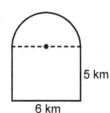

4 m

b)

5 km

6 km

Bonus ▶ Find the area of the parallelogram.

a)

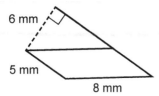

6 mm

5 mm

8 mm

b)

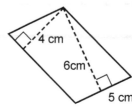

4 cm

6cm

5 cm

c)

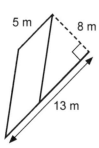

5 m   8 m

13 m

d)

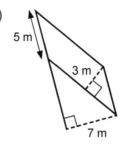

5 m

3 m

7 m

8. Will the fraction convert into a terminating or repeating decimal?

a) $\dfrac{58}{116}$

b) $\dfrac{9}{162}$

c) $\dfrac{3}{14\,570}$

9. Find 21% of 500 three different ways. Show your work.

10. Three of the four percentage problems below have the same answer. How can you tell which one is different without calculating the percentages? Which one is different?

A. 46% of 901 + 3% of 901

B. 52% of 901 + 3% of 901

C. 25% of 901 + 24% of 901

D. 52% of 901 − 3% of 901

SP7-1 Introduction to Probability

An **experiment** is an activity that has different possible results called **outcomes**. The set of all possible outcomes is called the **sample space**.

Example: If you roll a die, there are 6 possible **outcomes**: {1, 2, 3, 4, 5, and 6}.

1. List the possible outcomes in the sample space for the experiment.

   a) tossing a coin   _____   _____

   b) spinning the spinner   ____   ____   ____   ____

   c) choosing a vowel   ____   ____   ____   ____   ____   ____

   d) drawing a marble from a bag that contains 3 red, 1 blue, and 2 green marbles

   _____   _____   _____   _____   _____   _____

   e) choosing a letter from the word BATTLE

   ____   ____   ____   ____   ____   ____

   f) choosing a card with one of four suits from
      a deck of playing cards

   _____   _____   _____   _____

   g) choosing a weekday

   h) rolling a 4-sided die   ____   ____   ____   ____

   i) choosing a 3-letter short form for the months of the year

   _____   _____   _____   _____   _____   _____

   _____   _____   _____   _____   _____   _____

An **event** is a set of outcomes from the sample space.

Example: Events when you roll a die include:

- rolling an even number: {2, 4, 6}
- rolling a number less than 5: {1, 2, 3, 4}

2. You are rolling a die. Write the set of outcomes for the event.

a) rolling an odd number

_____

b) rolling a number greater than 3

_____

c) rolling a number greater than 6

_____

d) rolling a prime number

_____

3. You are choosing a letter from the word MATHEMATICS. Write the set of outcomes for the event.

a) the letter is a vowel

_____

b) the letter appears more than once in the word

_____

c) the letter is a consonant

_____

d) the printed letter has a curved line

_____

An event is **impossible** if none of its outcomes are in the sample space.
An event is **certain** if all of its outcomes are in the sample space.

Examples:

- Rolling a 7 with a die is impossible because 7 is not in the sample space.
- Rolling less than 7 with a die is certain because all the outcomes in the sample space are in the event.

Any other event is **in between** certain and impossible.

4. Is the event impossible (I), certain (C), or in between (B)?

a) rolling a 12 with a die   _____

b) rain falling tomorrow   _____

c) spinning red on a spinner that has red, blue, and green sections   _____

d) choosing a composite number from the list {32, 33, 34, 35, 36}   _____

e) choosing the letter "x" from the letters in the word PROBABILITY   _____

An outcome or event is **more likely** than another if it is expected to happen more often.

5. Is the spinner "more," "less," or "equally" likely to land on grey than white?

a)

_____

b)

_____

c)

_____

6. Write "more likely than," "less likely than," or "as likely as" in the blank.

a) Rolling a 2 with a die is _____ rolling a 5 with a die.

b) Choosing the winning ticket in a lottery is _____
tossing a quarter that lands on heads.

c) A day with sunshine is _____ a day with a hurricane.

d) Tossing a quarter that lands on heads is _____
tossing a quarter that lands on its edge.

You can use a probability line to show how likely an event is. The probability can vary from impossible to certain. An event that is equally likely to occur or not occur would appear at the midpoint of the probability line.

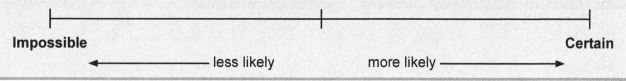

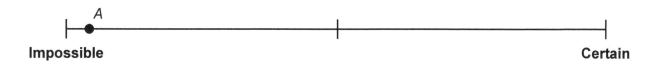

7. Mark a point on the line to show how likely the event is.

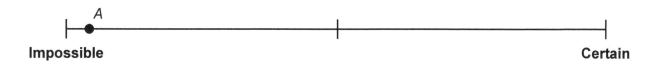

A. It will snow in Montreal in August.
B. It will be warm during the summer.
C. You get heads when tossing a coin.
D. The sun will rise in the east.
E. You draw a red card from a deck of cards.
F. You win a prize in a raffle.

8. For the experiment of rolling a die, describe four events: 1 certain, 1 impossible, and 2 in between. Place them on a probability line and explain how you place the events.

SP7-2 Representations of Probability

> In an experiment, the outcomes in an event are known as **favourable outcomes**.

1. The sample space when rolling a die is {1, 2, 3, 4, 5, 6}. List the set of favourable outcomes for the event.

    a) rolling a number greater than 4

    _____

    c) rolling a prime number

    _____

    b) rolling an even number

    _____

    d) rolling a 7

    _____

2. List the set of favourable outcomes for the event when spinning the spinner.

    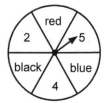

    a) spinning a colour

    _____

    c) spinning an even number

    _____

    b) spinning a number

    _____

    d) spinning a colour with 4 letters

    _____

> The probability of an event tells you how likely the event is to occur. It is the ratio of the number of favourable outcomes to all outcomes.
>
> $$P(\text{event}) = \text{favourable outcomes : all outcomes}$$
>
> If all the outcomes are equally likely, $P(\text{event}) = \dfrac{\text{\# favourable outcomes}}{\text{\# outcomes}}$

3. The outcomes for rolling a die are {1, 2, 3, 4, 5, 6}. Complete the table. Use the number of outcomes to write the probability of each event as a fraction in lowest terms.

	Event	Favourable Outcomes	Probability
a)	rolling an even number	{2, 4, 6}	$P(\text{even}) = \dfrac{3}{6} = \dfrac{1}{2}$
b)	rolling greater than 2		$P(> 2) =$
c)	rolling less than 3		$P(< 3) =$
d)	rolling a prime number		$P(\text{prime}) =$
e)	rolling a factor of 12		$P(\text{factor of 12}) =$

4. Find the probability of the event when selecting a card from a standard deck of cards. Write the answer as a ratio in lowest terms.

	Event	# Outcomes	Probability
a)	choosing a heart	13	P(♥) = 13 : 52 = 1 : 4
b)	choosing a 7		P(7) =
c)	choosing a face card		P(face) =
d)	choosing a black suit		P(black) =

5. In Question 4, which is more likely to occur: choosing a 7 or choosing a face card? Explain.

6. Use the number of degrees for each section to find the probability of each event as a fraction in lowest terms.

	Event	Favourable Outcomes	Probability
a)	spinning green	{G}	P(G) = $\frac{45}{360}$ = $\frac{1}{8}$
b)	spinning red		P(R) =
c)	spinning a number		P(number) =
d)	spinning a colour		P(colour) =

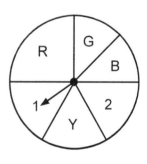

7. Explain why we shouldn't use the number of sections to find the probability in Question 6.

8. Use the number of sections in the spinner to find the probability of the event written as a percentage.

	Event	Favourable Outcomes	Probability
a)	spinning 3	{3}	$P(3) = \dfrac{1}{4} = 0.25 = 25\%$
b)	spinning an odd number		$P(\text{odd}) =$
c)	spinning an even number		$P(\text{even}) =$
d)	spinning a 4		$P(4) =$
e)	spinning less than 7		$P(< 7) =$

> The probability of a certain event is 1. The probability of an impossible event is 0.

9. State whether the probability of the event is 0 or 1.

	Event	Prob			Event	Prob
a)	rolling a 7 using a die	_____		d)	the sun sets in the west	_____
b)	tomorrow has 24 hours	_____		e)	a dog flies like a bird	_____
c)	rolling < 2 using a pair of dice	_____		f)	the Earth revolves around the Sun	_____

10. Describe 3 events for the experiment: one with probability 0, one with probability 1, and one that is in between.

a) spinning a spinner with 4 equal sections for red, red, green, and blue

b) choosing a card from a deck of cards

SP7-3 Probability of an Event Not Occurring

1. When rolling a die, the sample space is {1, 2, 3, 4, 5, 6}.

    a) Use the number of outcomes in the event to find the probability.

    i) $P(1) = \dfrac{1}{6}$

    ii) $P(2) =$

    iii) $P(3) =$

    iv) $P(4) =$

    v) $P(5) =$

    vi) $P(6) =$

    b) Find the sum of the probabilities in parts i) through vi).

2. A bag contains 2 red, 3 green, 1 yellow, and 4 blue marbles.

    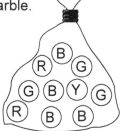

    a) Use the number of marbles to find the probability of selecting the marble.
    Write your answer as a decimal.

    i) $P(\text{red}) = \dfrac{2}{10} = 0.2$

    ii) $P(\text{green}) =$

    iii) $P(\text{blue}) =$

    iv) $P(\text{yellow}) =$

    b) Find the sum of the probabilities in parts i) through iv).

3. A deck of 52 cards has 13 clubs, 13 diamonds, 13 hearts, and 13 spades.

    a) Use the number of cards in each suit to find the probability of selecting the suit.
    Write your answer as a percentage.

    i) $P(\text{clubs}) = \dfrac{13}{52} = 0.25 = 25\%$

    ii) $P(\text{diamonds}) =$

    iii) $P(\text{hearts}) =$

    iv) $P(\text{spades}) =$

    b) Find the sum of the probabilities in parts i) through iv).

4. Looking at your answers to Questions 1 to 3, what can you conclude about the sum of the probabilities of the outcomes in a sample space?

The probability that an event doesn't occur is 1 minus the probability that the event does occur.

P(event does not occur) = 1 − P(event occurs)

5. The Venn diagram shows the responses of 50 people who were asked their favourite colour.

a) Find the probability that a person chose a colour as their favourite.

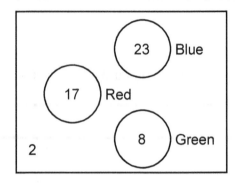

Colour	Probability
red	$P(R) = \dfrac{17}{50} = 0.34$
blue	
green	
no colour chosen	

b) Find the probability that a person chose a favourite colour.

c) Show that P(no colour chosen) = 1 − P(colour chosen).

6. Salvina picks a card from a deck of cards.

a) Find the probability that she chooses a heart. _____

b) Find the probability that she doesn't choose a heart. _____

7. Boris rolls a die.

a) Find the probability that he rolls a 1, 2, 3, or 4. _____

b) Find 1 minus the probability that he rolls a 5 or 6. _____

8. Lucinda spins a spinner with an unknown number of sections and colours. The probability that she spins a red is $\dfrac{3}{4}$. Find the probability that she doesn't spin a red.

9. In 2012, the probability of a Canadian adult aged 20 or older having a heart attack was 2.1%. What was the probability that an adult aged 20 or older did not have a heart attack?

10. In a Canadian lottery, the probability of winning any prize is approximately 5 : 33. What is the probability of not winning a prize? Write your answer as a ratio.

11. A survey shows that the probability of owning at least one cat is 82%.

    a) If you don't own at least one cat, how many cats do you own?

    b) What is the probability of not owning a cat?

12. The probability that a driver never has an accident is 0.23.

    a) For the event "never has an accident," what does it mean if the event does not occur?

    b) What is the probability of having at least one accident?

13. The probability of tossing two coins and getting no heads is $\frac{1}{4}$. Find the probability of tossing two coins and getting at least 1 head.

14. When rolling a pair of dice, the probability of rolling less than 7 is $\frac{15}{36}$. The probability of rolling greater than 7 is also $\frac{15}{36}$. Find the probability of rolling exactly 7.

15. When tossing 3 coins, the probability that you will get 3 heads is $\frac{1}{8}$. The probability that you will get 3 tails is also $\frac{1}{8}$. Find the probability of getting either 2 heads and a tail or 2 tails and a head.

16. In the casino game roulette, a ball rolls around a large wheel until it falls into one of 38 pockets coloured red, black, or green. The probability of the ball landing on red is $\frac{9}{19}$. The probability of the ball landing on black is $\frac{9}{19}$. How many sections are coloured green?

SP7-4 Independent Events

Two events are **independent** if the occurrence of one event does not affect the probability of the occurrence of the other event. The events may occur simultaneously or at different times.

Example: When rolling a pair of dice, the number rolled on the first die does not affect the number rolled on the second die. So, rolling a pair of dice are independent events.

1. State whether the events are dependent (D) or independent (I).

   a) rolling a die and selecting a card from a deck _____

   b) not doing the laundry and running out of clean clothes _____

   c) owning a dog and having blonde hair _____

   d) being the first person to enter a movie theatre and finding a good seat _____

   e) tossing heads with one coin and then tossing tails with a different coin _____

   f) tossing two coins at the same time and getting heads on both _____

2. A bag contains 7 red marbles and 3 green marbles.

   a) Find the probability of choosing a red marble from the bag. _____

   b) After the event in part a), the marble is replaced. Now find the probability of choosing a green marble from the bag. _____

   c) After the event in part a), the marble is not replaced. Now find the probability of choosing a green marble from the bag. _____

   d) Explain why choosing a red marble and replacing it, then choosing a green marble are independent events.

   e) Explain why choosing a red marble and not replacing it, then choosing a green marble are dependent events.

3. Two cards are chosen from a deck of cards without replacement. Explain why the events of choosing a jack and then an ace without replacement are dependent events.

Tossing a coin and then spinning a spinner with sections 1, 2, and 3 are independent events.
Tree diagrams can be used to list all the outcomes for two or more events.

Step 1: Write the outcomes for the first event.

Step 2: Under each outcome for the first event, write the outcomes for the second event.

Step 3: To list the outcomes, follow any path from the top of the tree to the bottom.

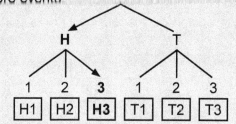

The highlighted path shows the outcome of tossing a head and then spinning a 3.

4. Complete the tree diagram to show all the outcomes for the independent events.

   a) tossing a coin, then rolling a 4-sided die

   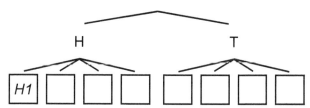

   b) spinning a spinner with equal sections R, G, and Y, then tossing a coin

   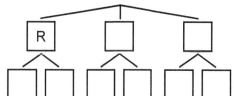

5. The menu shows the options for breakfast at a restaurant. Complete the tree diagram to show the possible breakfasts you can order.

   Main Course:
   Eggs (E), Toast (T), Pancakes (P)

   Drinks:
   Coffee (C), Juice (J), Milk (M)

   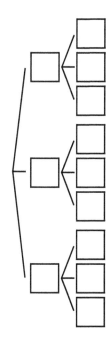

6. a) Use Questions 4 and 5 to complete the table.

Question	# Branches at 1ˢᵗ Level	# Branches at 2ⁿᵈ Level	# Outcomes
4. a)			
4. b)			
5.			

   b) How can we use the number of branches at each level to predict the total number of outcomes?

Statistics and Probability 7-4

73

Tables can be used to list the outcomes of two events. The **column headings** show the outcomes of the first event. The **row headings** show the outcomes of the second event.

Example: A coin is tossed. Then a spinner with equal sections 1, 2, and 3 is spun.

	H	T
1	H1	T1
2	H2	T2
3	H3	T3

→ T2 in the table shows the outcome tossing tails followed by spinning a 2.

7. Filomena tosses two coins. Complete the table to show the possible outcomes.

	H	T
H		
T		

a) What is the total number of possible outcomes? _____

b) How many of the outcomes have one head and one tail? _____

8. Tyrell tosses a coin and then spins the spinner. Complete the table to show the possible outcomes.

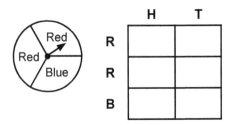

	H	T
R		
R		
B		

a) What is the total number of possible outcomes? _____

b) How many outcomes have red? _____

9. Shakir rolls two dice and finds the total.

a) Complete the table to record the possible outcomes.

b) How many possible outcomes are there? _____

c) How many outcomes have the total 8? _____

d) How many outcomes have the total 5? _____

e) How many outcomes have a total less than 3? _____

f) Which total occurs the most often? _____

g) How many distinct totals are there? _____

	1	2	3	4	5	6
1					6	
2		4				
3				7		
4						
5						
6		8				

10. A 6-sided die and a 9-sided die are rolled.

a) How many possible outcomes are there? _____

b) How many outcomes will have the total 2? _____

SP7-5 Probability of Independent Events

To find the probability of independent events, use a tree diagram, table, or list to find all the possible outcomes. Then find the ratio of favourable outcomes to possible outcomes.

Example: A coin is tossed, then a spinner with equal sections Red, Red, Yellow is spun.
Find the probability of the outcome Heads, Red

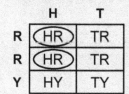

	H	T
R	HR	TR
R	HR	TR
Y	HY	TY

There are 2 favourable outcomes
There are 6 possible outcomes.

$$P(HR) = \frac{2}{6} = \frac{1}{3}$$

1. Mirko spins the two spinners. Complete the tree diagram, then find the probability of spinning at least 1 red.

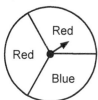 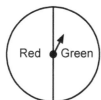 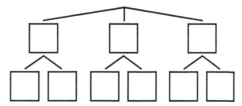

P(at least one red) = _____

2. Use the table to list the possible outcomes when Pietra spins the spinners.

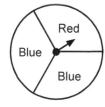 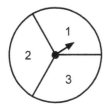

	R	B	B
1			
2			
3			

a) Find the probability that blue and an odd number were spun.

_____

b) Find the probability that red and an even number were spun.

_____

3. Calista tossed a coin, then spun a spinner with the equal sections 1, 2, 3, and 5.

a) Find all the possible outcomes.   H: H1, H2, _____, _____

T: T1, _____, _____, _____

b) Find the probability that the coin was a head and that an odd number was spun.

---

4. Viktor rolls two dice.

a) Shade the squares showing the favourable outcomes for the event. Write the probability as a fraction in lowest terms.

   i) rolls a sum of 6

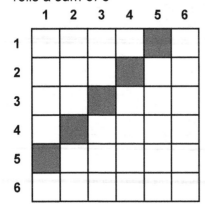

        P(6) = _____

   ii) rolls a sum of 8

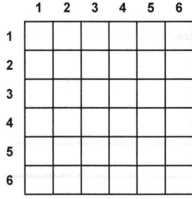

        P(8) = _____

   iii) rolls a sum of 5

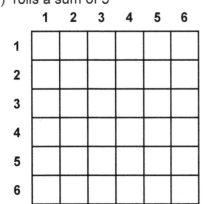

        P(5) = _____

   iv) rolls a sum of 7

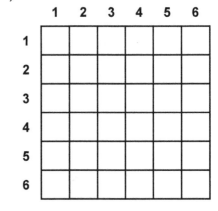

        P(7) = _____

b) When Viktor rolls the pair of dice, find...

   i) the total as likely to occur as an 8. _____

   ii) the total as likely to occur as a 5. _____

   iii) the probability of rolling 13. _____

   iv) the probability of rolling 2. _____

   v) the probability of not rolling 2. _____

   vi) the probability of rolling 3. _____

   vii) the probability of not rolling 3. _____

5. Some board games use tetrahedral dice. Each die has 4 triangular sides with the numbers 1, 2, 3, and 4.

   a) Complete the table to find all the possible outcomes when rolling a pair of tetrahedral dice.

   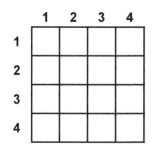

	1	2	3	4
1				
2				
3				
4				

   b) Which totals are least likely to occur? _____ _____

   c) Which total is most likely to occur? _____

   d) Find the probability of the event. Write the answer as a fraction in lowest terms.

   i) rolling a sum of 5   ii) rolling a 3

   iii) rolling an even total   iv) rolling a total greater than 3

6. You can create a die that behaves like a 3-sided die by renaming the sides on a 6-sided die. Replace the 6 with a 3, replace the 5 with a 2, and replace the 4 with a 1.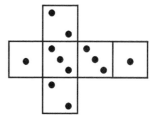

   a) Complete the list to find all the possible outcomes of rolling a pair of 3-sided dice.

   1: *1 – 1*   *1 – 2*   *1 – 3*   2: _____ _____ _____   3: _____ _____ _____

   b) What total is most likely to occur? _____

   c) What totals are least likely to occur? _____ _____

   d) Find the probability of rolling the totals. Write the answer as a fraction in lowest terms.

   i) rolling a 3   ii) rolling a 4   iii) rolling an even number

SP7-6 Experimental Probability

> **Theoretical probability** tells us how likely an event is to occur if we were to perform the experiment.
>
> Example: When rolling a die, P(rolling greater than 4) = $\frac{2}{6}$
>
> For every 6 times we perform the experiment, we expect to roll greater than 4 two times.
>
> We can use the theoretical probability to predict the number of favourable outcomes in an actual experiment.
>
> Example: Juanita rolls a die 300 times. Predict the number of times she rolls the number 5.
>
> **Step 1:** Find the theoretical probability as a percentage. $P(5) = \frac{1}{6} \approx 16.7\%$
>
> **Step 2:** Multiply by the number of experiments. Prediction = $16.7\% \times 300 \approx 50$

1. Use the theoretical probability to predict the actual number of outcomes.

   a) Viola spun the spinner 400 times.
   Predict the number of times red will be spun.

   b) Xander rolled a tetrahedral die 300 times.
   Predict the number of times the roll was greater than 3.

   c) Alessandra rolled a 3-sided die 150 times.
   Predict the number of times an even number was rolled.

   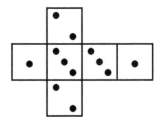

   d) Nik rolled a pair of dice 750 times.
   Shade the table to help predict.

   i) How many times was the number 7 rolled?

   ii) How many times was either a 2 or a 12 rolled?

   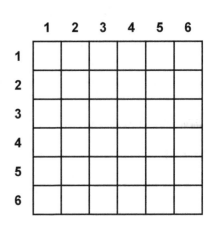

	1	2	3	4	5	6
1						
2						
3						
4						
5						
6						

When you perform an experiment, the **experimental probability** is the ratio of the number of times an outcome occurs to the number of trials.

experimental probability = $\dfrac{\text{\# times outcome occurs}}{\text{\# trials}}$

Dahlia tossed a coin 500 times. She recorded 243 tails and 257 heads.

EP(tails) = $\dfrac{243}{500}$ = 0.486   EP(heads) = $\dfrac{257}{500}$ = 0.514

2. Leda tossed a die 120 times and recorded the results.

1	2	3	4	5	6
18	16	23	17	24	22

   a) Find the experimental probability of rolling a 3 in Leda's experiment, accurate to 3 decimal digits.

   b) Find the theoretical probability of rolling a 3 with a die accurate to 3 decimal digits.

   c) Are the answers to parts a) and b) the same? Explain.

   d) If Leda performed the experiment another 120 times, do you think she would roll the number three 23 times again? Explain.

3. Rinaldo chose a single card from a deck of cards, each time with replacement, and recorded the results.

♣	♦	♥	♠
74	81	77	68

   a) Find the number of times the experiment was performed.

   b) Find the experimental probability of choosing a spade.

   c) Find the theoretical probability of choosing a spade from a deck of cards.

   d) Are the answers to parts b) and c) the same? Explain.

   e) If Rinaldo performed the experiment another 300 times, do you think he would choose a spade exactly 68 times again? Explain.

4. A spinner has 4 equal sections. Two of the sections are red, one is green, and one is blue. Jamari, Taniqua, and Dimitri use a spreadsheet to simulate spinning the spinner and recorded the results.

a) Find the theoretical probability of spinning red.

	Total	R	G	B
Jamari	240	124	59	57
Taniqua	1500	748	375	377
Dimitri	15 000	7490	3748	3762

b) Find the experimental probability of rolling a red for each student.

c) Are the experimental probabilities in part c) equal to the theoretical probability? Explain.

d) As the number of experiments increases, what appears to happen when comparing the theoretical and experimental probabilities?

For some experiments, the theoretical probability is difficult to calculate. We can use the experimental probability to predict the number of favourable outcomes.

A baseball player got 27 hits in 91 times at bat. Predict how many hits she will get in 320 times at bat.

Step 1: Find the experimental probability as a decimal. $EP(hits) = \dfrac{27}{91} \approx 0.297$

Step 2: Multiply by the number of experiments. $Prediction = 0.297 \times 320 \approx 95$

---

5. Use the experimental probability to predict the results of the experiment.

a) Fredo spun a spinner with unequal sections and recorded the results. Predict the number of times red will appear if he spins 750 times.

R	G	B
195	52	53

b) Giselle chose marbles with replacement from a bag containing an unknown number of different coloured marbles. After 270 experiments, they recorded 183 blue, 42 green, and 45 red marbles. Predict the number of times they will choose a red marble if they repeat the experiment 900 times.

c) A car company sold 25 red, 36 blue, and 85 silver cars of a particular model in January. The company expects to sell 1600 cars of that model from February through December. How many cars of each colour should they manufacture for the remainder of the year?

d) A cellphone manufacturer made 50 000 phones last month. After inspecting 1500 phones, the manufacturer found that 23 were defective. If you purchase a phone from this manufacturer, what is the probability that you get a defective phone? Predict how many customers will buy defective phones if the manufacturer sells 85 000 next month.

SS7-22 Angles

We measure angles in **degrees**. Example: This angle measures 1 degree — 1°.

A right angle measures 90°. A straight angle measures 180°.

1. Identify the angle as "less than 90°" or "more than 90°."

a)

less than 90°

b)

_____

c)

_____

Acute angles are less than a right angle. They measure between 0° and 90°. **Obtuse angles** are greater than a right angle and smaller than a straight angle. They measure between 90° and 180°.

2. Identify the angle as "acute" or "obtuse."

a)

_____

b)

_____

c)

_____

3. Does the angle measure describe an "acute" or "obtuse" angle?

a) 55° _____

b) 130° _____

c) 66° _____

d) 93° _____

e) 178° _____

f) 19° _____

To measure an angle, use a **protractor**.

A protractor has 180 subdivisions of 1° around its curved side.

It has two scales, so you can measure angles starting from either side.

0°   180°

4. Identify the angle as "acute" or "obtuse." Circle the two numbers that the top arm of the angle passes through. Choose the correct angle measure.

a)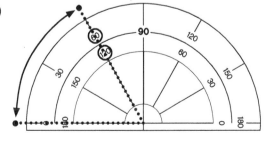

The angle is ___acute___.

The angle measures ___60°___.

b)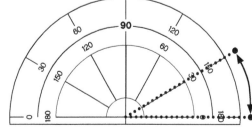

The angle is _____.

The angle measures _____.

Shape and Space 7-22   81

5. Identify the angle as "acute" or "obtuse." Then write the measure of the angle.

a)

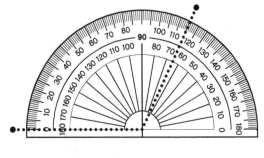

_____, _____

b)

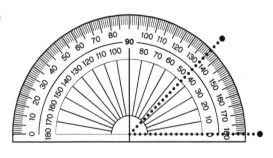

_____, _____

c)

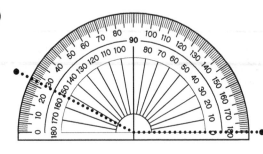

_____, _____

d)

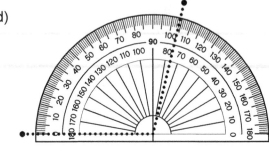

_____, _____

Each protractor has a **base line** and an **origin**.

To measure an angle, line up the base line of the protractor with one arm of the angle.

Place the origin of the protractor on the vertex of the angle.

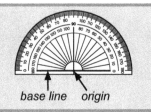

base line   origin

---

6. a) In which picture is the protractor placed correctly? _____

A.

B.

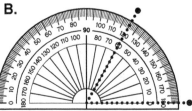

C.

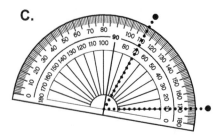

b) What is wrong with the other pictures?

---

7. Measure the angle using a protractor. Extend the arms if needed.

a)

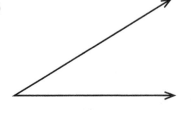

_____

b)

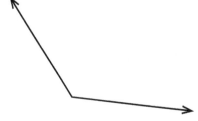

_____

c)

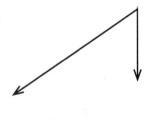

_____

8. Use the grid to estimate the angle. Then measure the angle to check your estimate.

a)

Estimate: _____

Actual: _____

b)

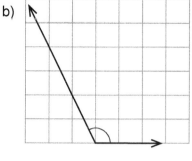

Estimate: _____

Actual: _____

c)

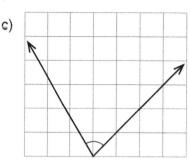

Estimate: _____

Actual: _____

d)

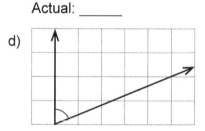

Estimate: _____

Actual: _____

e)

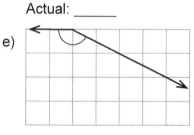

Estimate: _____

Actual: _____

Bonus ▶

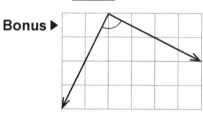

Estimate: _____

Actual: _____

9. Estimate the measure of the angle. Then use a protractor to check your estimate.

a)

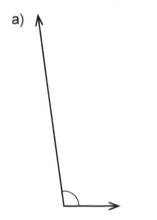

Estimate: _____

Actual: _____

b)

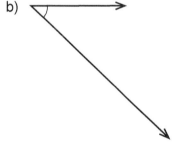

Estimate: _____

Actual: _____

c)

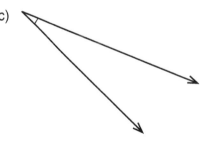

Estimate: _____

Actual: _____

 10. The large angle is divided into equal angles. Estimate the size of the small angles. Explain how you know.

a)

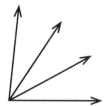

b)

c)

SS7-23 Angle Bisectors and Central Angles

When naming angles the vertex letter is always in the middle.

∠XYZ or ∠ZYX, not ∠YXZ and not ∠XZY

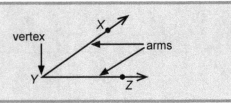

1. Circle the vertex. Name the angle.

a)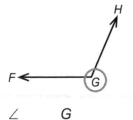

∠ _G_ ___ ___

b)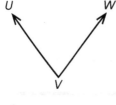

∠ ___ ___ ___

c)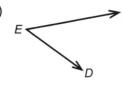

∠ ___ ___ ___

d)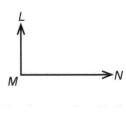

∠ ___ ___ ___

An **angle bisector** divides an angle into two equal angles.

Use hash marks to show equal angles.

AD bisects ∠BAC, so ∠BAD = ∠CAD.

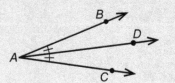

2. AD bisects ∠CAB. What are the measures of the two angles?

a)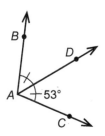

∠BAD = _____

∠BAC = _____

b)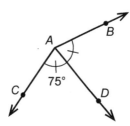

∠BAD = _____

∠BAC = _____

c)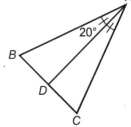

∠CAD = _____

∠BAC = _____

3. A **diagonal** in a polygon is a line segment that joins two vertices that are not adjacent.

a) Is the diagonal of the rectangle shown an angle bisector?

Prediction: yes / no

b) Check by measuring. Was your prediction correct? yes / no

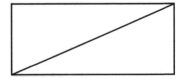

4. Use a protractor to draw the bisector of the angle.

a)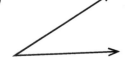

b)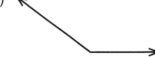

c)

An angle that has its vertex at the centre of a circle is called a **central angle** for that circle.

5. a) Sort the angles into the Venn diagram.

∠SAB, ∠SBA, ∠ASB, ∠QAR, ∠CRA, ∠TBQ, ∠QAC

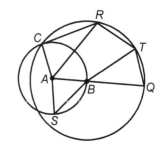

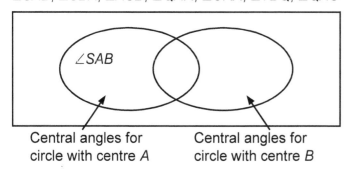

Central angles for   Central angles for
circle with centre *A*   circle with centre *B*

b) If possible, add another angle to each region of the Venn diagram. If no angle can be added to one of the regions, explain why.

6. *H* is the centre of the circle.

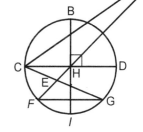

a) *HA* bisects the angle ∠BHD. What is the measure of the central angles in degrees?

∠AHD = _____   ∠CHF = _____   ∠FHI = _____

∠FHD = _____   ∠BHC = _____

b) To find the sum of the central angles, use angles that cover the entire rotation around the centre of the circle but do not overlap. What is the sum of the central angles in this diagram?

∠BHC + ∠FHC + ∠FHD + ∠DHB = _____ + _____ + _____ + _____ = _____

c) Find the sum of the central angles using a different set of angles.

∠AHC + ∠AHI + _____ = _____

d) Does the sum of the central angles depend on the angles used to find it? _____

7. A circle is divided into six equal parts. What is the measure of central angle *AOB*? How do you know?

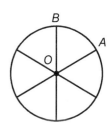

Shape and Space 7-23

SS7-24 Properties of Rhombuses and Isosceles Triangles

1. The diagram shows a rhombus.

   a) Mark the equal line segments and the equal angles.

   b) Mark the right angles.

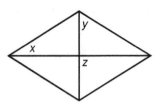

2. In the diagrams below, the centres of two circles are joined by a line segment.

   A.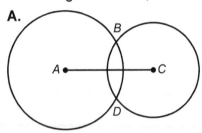

   B.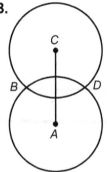

   C.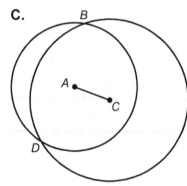

   D.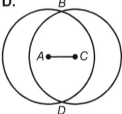

   E.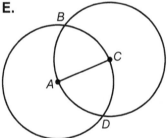

   F.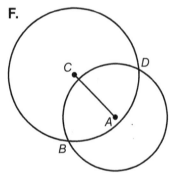

   a) Predict in which diagrams *ABCD* is a rhombus. Explain your thinking.

   b) Construct the quadrilaterals *ABCD* and check your predictions.

3. a) Use a ruler to construct an isosceles triangle with angle *M*.

   b) Use a ruler to construct a bisector of angle *M*.

4. The circles have centres *S* or *T*. Does the diagram contain angle bisectors? Which lines are angle bisectors? Which angles do they bisect? How do you know?

   a)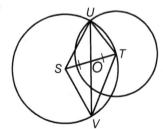

   b)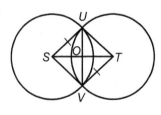

   Bonus ▶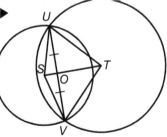

SS7-25 Parallel and Perpendicular Lines

1. a) Are line segments *AB* and *AC* equal? Are line segments *DB* and *DC* equal?
   Measure to check. If yes, mark them as equal on the diagram.

   i) 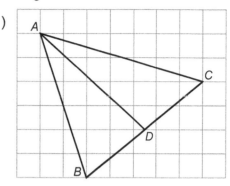   ii)

   b) Is *AD* perpendicular to *BC*? Use a protractor to check. If yes, show that on the diagram in part a).

   c) Is *AD* the perpendicular bisector of *BC*?

   i) _____   ii) _____

2. Identify the equal line segments and the right angles. All circles have radius 3 m.
   L and *N* are the centres of the circles.

   a) 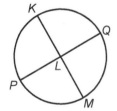   b) 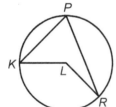   c) 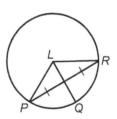   d)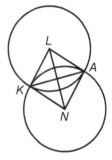

REMINDER: The sum of the angles in any triangle is 180°.

---

3. *ABC* is an equilateral triangle. Solve the following without a protractor.

   a) What is the angle measure of each angle in *ABC*? _____

   b) Use a ruler to construct a perpendicular bisector *AD* of the side *BC*.

   c) Calculate and mark the measure of every angle in the diagram.

   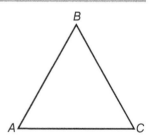

4. Are the lines parallel? Check by using a protractor to construct a perpendicular line.

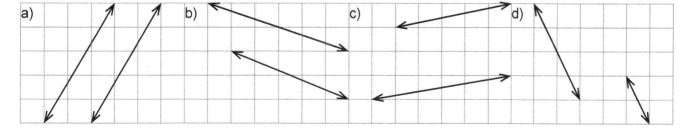

SS7-26 Introduction to Constructions

An **arc** is an unbroken part of a circle. The centre of the circle is also the centre of the arc. Use an arc when you only need a small part of a circle.

Two arcs with the same centre
and different radii

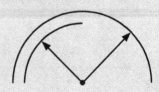

Two arcs with different centres
and the same radii.

1. The centre of an arc is the point where you put the point of the compass to draw the arc.
   Circle the point that is the centre of the arc.

   a)

   b)

   c)

2. Construct an arc with centre O through point A. Is point B on the arc? Extend the arc
   to find out.

   a) A   B   b)   O   A   c)   O   A

   O   B   B

   _____   _____   _____

3. The arcs are centred at points A and B. Use a compass to extend each arc into a full
   circle. How many intersection points do these circles have?

   a)

   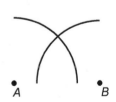

   b)

   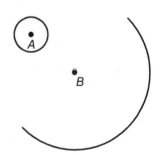

   c)

   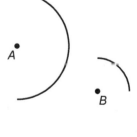

   _____   _____   _____

Use a compass to create a line segment *CD* equal to a line segment *AB*.

Step 1. Set the compass to the width of *AB*.

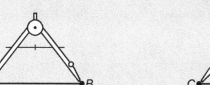

Step 2: Without changing the setting of the compass, set the point of the compass at *C*.

Step 3: Construct a little arc intersecting the line. Label the intersection point *D*.

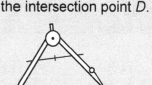

4. Use a compass to construct two line segments, *CD* and *CE*, equal to the line segment *AB* along the given line or rays. Check your work with a ruler.

a)

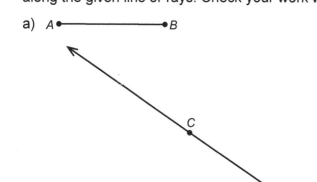

b)

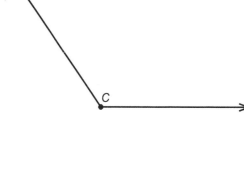

5. a) Draw two arcs with radius *AB* centred at *B* and *C*. Extend the arcs enough that they intersect at two points.

i)

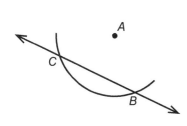

ii)

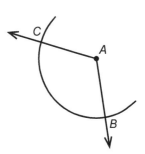

b) What do you notice about the location of *A*?

6. In Question 5, *A* is the centre of the given arc.

a) What kind of triangle is *ABC* in both parts i) and ii) of Question 5? How do you know?

b) Label the second intersection point of the arcs centred at *B* and *C* in Question 5 as point *D*. Construct the quadrilateral *ABDC*. What kind of quadrilateral have you constructed? Explain.

SS7-27 Straightedge and Compass Constructions I

To construct a bisector of ∠Q:

Step 1: Draw an arc centred at the vertex of angle Q. Label the intersection points with the arms T and S.

Step 2: Without changing the setting of the compass, draw a small arc as shown centred at S.

Step 3: Without changing the setting of the compass, draw a small arc as shown centred at T. Label the intersection point of the arcs U.

Step 4: Construct a line QU. This is the bisector of the angle.

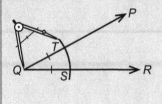 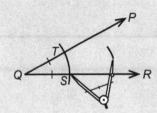 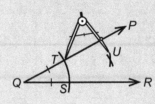 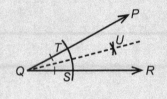

1. a) Use a compass to construct B on one arm and D other so that AB = AD.

   b) Use a compass to construct a point C (different from A) so that BC = CD = AB.

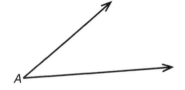 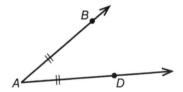

   c) Draw the angle bisector of ∠A on the diagram in part b).

2. Complete Steps 2 to 4 from the method above to construct the angle bisector of ∠Q.

3. Bisect ∠Q.

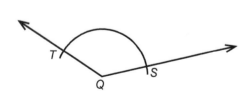 

4. The diagram is from Step 4 above.

   a) Construct line segments TU and SU. Label all the equal line segments in the diagram.

   b) What type of quadrilateral is QTUS? _____

   c) How do you know that QU bisects ∠TQS?

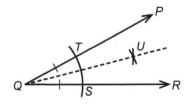

To construct a perpendicular bisector of a line segment *AB*:

Step 1: Construct an arc centred at *A* with radius larger than half the distance *AB*.

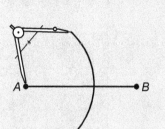

Step 2: Construct another arc, centred at *B*, with the same radius as the first arc. Extend the arcs so they intersect in two points.

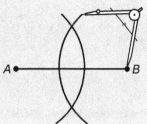

Step 3: Construct a line through the intersection points of the two arcs. This is the perpendicular bisector of *AB*.

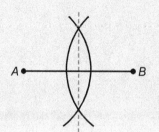

5. Construct the perpendicular bisector of the line segment.

a)

b)

6. The diagram is from Step 3 in the method above.

   a) Label the intersection points of the arcs *C* and *D*. Construct line segments *AC*, *AD*, *BC*, and *BD*. Label all the equal line segments in the diagram.

   b) What type of quadrilateral is *ACBD*? _____

   c) Label all the right angles in the diagram.

   d) How do you know that *CD* is a perpendicular bisector of *AB*?

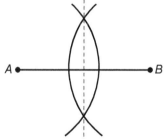

7. Use a compass and a straightedge.

   a) Construct a line segment *EF*. Then construct a perpendicular bisector of *EF*. Label the intersection of *EF* and the perpendicular bisector, *G*.

   b) Construct line segment *GH* on the perpendicular bisector of *EF* so that *GH* = *GE*. Construct the line segment *EH*.

   c) Bisect ∠*EGH*. Extend it to intersect *EH* and label the intersection point *I*.

   d) What can you say about *IE*, *IH*, and angles *GIH* and *GIE*? What is the relationship between *GI* and *EH*?

SS7-28 Straightedge and Compass Constructions II

To construct a line perpendicular to line *n* through point *C*, which is on line *n*:

Step 1: Put the compass point on *C*. Construct an arc intersecting line *n* at points *D* and *E*.

Step 2: Construct the perpendicular bisector *FG* of the line segment *DE*.

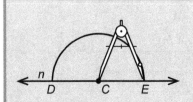

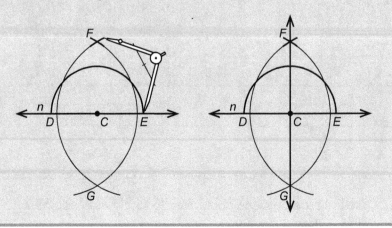

1. a) What can you say about line segments *CE* and *CD* in the diagram above?

   b) *C* is the _____ of the line segment *DE*.

   c) Explain why *FG* intersects *DE* exactly at point *C*.

2. Construct a line perpendicular to the given line through *C*.

   a)

   b)

   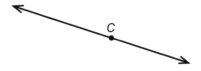

3. a) Construct an arc centred at *P* such that it intersects line *m* in two points: *H* and *J*.

   b) Set the compass to a width greater than *PH*. Construct an arc centred at *H* and an arc centred at *J* such that they have the same radius and intersect at one point. Label the point of intersection *K*.

   c) What kind of triangle is *KHJ*? _____

   d) Construct line segment *KP*. Explain why it is perpendicular to *m*.

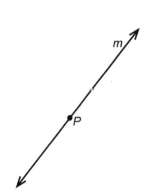

To construct a line perpendicular to line *n* through a point *C* not on *n*:

Step 1: Construct an arc with centre *C* intersecting *n* at points *D* and *E*.

Step 2: Using the same setting of the compass, construct an arc centred at *D* with radius *CD* as shown.

Step 3: Using the same setting of the compass, construct an arc centred at *E* with radius *CE* such that the arcs from Steps 2 and 3 intersect. Label the intersection point *F*.

Step 4: Construct the line *CF*. It is perpendicular to *n*.

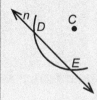 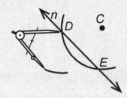 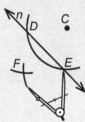 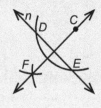

4. Construct the line through point *C* that is perpendicular to line *m*.

a)

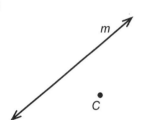

b)

5. The diagram shows Step 4 of the above method for constructing a perpendicular line.

a) Construct the quadrilateral *CDFE*. What kind of quadrilateral is *CDFE*? Explain.

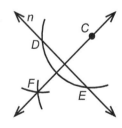

b) Explain why *CF* is perpendicular to line *n*.

6. a) Construct a line *m* perpendicular to *k* through point *P*.

b) Construct a line *n* perpendicular to *m* through point *P*.

c) What do you know about lines *k* and *n*? Explain.

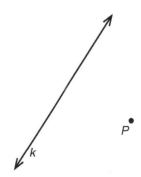

SS7-29 Constructions: Problems and Puzzles

1. Construct a rectangle *ABCD* such that the given points *A* and *C* are its opposite vertices.

   a) Use a ruler and protractor.   b) Use a compass and straightedge.

2. Construct a square *PQRS* such that one of its sides is on line *m*.

   a) Use a ruler and protractor.   b) Use a compass and straightedge.

   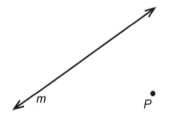   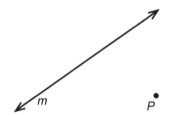

3. Bisect the angle.

   a) Use a ruler.   b) Use a protractor.   c) Use a compass and straightedge.

   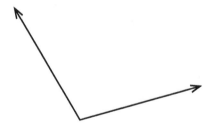   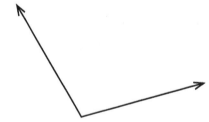   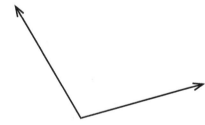

4. Construct the perpendicular bisector of line segment *AB*.

   a) Use a ruler and protractor.   b) Use a compass and straightedge.

SP7-7 Frequency Tables and Circle Graphs

The **frequency** of a value is the number of times it occurs in a data set.

Example: 1, 0, 1, 1, 2, 1, 1, 0, 1, 0 ⟶

Data Value	Frequency
0	|||
1	⅏|
2	|

A **frequency table** (left table below) shows how many times a data value occurs in a set. The **relative frequency** (right table below) of a data value is its frequency divided by the total number of data values.

Data Value	Frequency
0	3
1	6
2	1

Data Value	Relative Frequency
0	$\frac{3}{10}$
1	$\frac{6}{10}$
2	$\frac{1}{10}$

1. a) Transfer the data into the tally chart. Cross out each number as you mark it in the chart.

i) 0̶, 3̶, 2̶, 0̶, 2̶, 2̶, 3̶

Data Value	Frequency
0	//
1	
2	///
3	//

ii) 4̶, 3̶, 1, 4, 3, 3, 1, 4, 4, 3, 4, 4

Data Value	Frequency
1	
2	
3	/
4	/

iii) 2, 5, 5, 5, 2, 2, 2, 2, 5

Data Value	Frequency
2	
3	
4	
5	

b) How many numbers are in the data set? i) __7__ ii) _____ iii) _____

c) How many tallies are in the frequency column? i) __7__ ii) _____ iii) _____

d) If your answers to parts b) and c) aren't the same, find your mistake.

e) Complete the table to show the frequency and relative frequency for part ii) in part a).

Data Value	Frequency	Relative Frequency
1	2	$\frac{2}{12}$
2	0	
3		
4		

Statistics and Probability 7-7

95

2. Write the fraction as an equivalent fraction over 100 and then as a percentage.

a) $\dfrac{3}{10} = \dfrac{30}{100} = 30\%$

b) $\dfrac{9}{20} = \dfrac{\quad}{100} = \quad\%$

c) $\dfrac{13}{50} = \dfrac{\quad}{100} = \quad\%$

d) $\dfrac{10}{25} = \dfrac{\quad}{100} = \quad\%$

e) $\dfrac{18}{30} = \dfrac{6}{10} = \dfrac{\quad}{100} = \quad\%$

f) $\dfrac{28}{80} = \dfrac{\quad}{20} = \dfrac{\quad}{100} = \quad\%$

Sam surveyed 50 students in his school about their favourite genre of movie.

He used a circle graph to display his results.

Movie Genre	Frequency	Percentage
Action	20	40%
Comedy	15	30%
Horror	5	10%
Other	10	20%

Circle graphs can be used to show a visual representation of data.

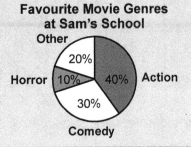

Favourite Movie Genres at Sam's School

---

3. By only looking at the above graph, which of the three known movie genres is the least liked by students in Sam's school? How do you know?

4. a) What percentage of students like each genre of movie in each school? Complete the chart.

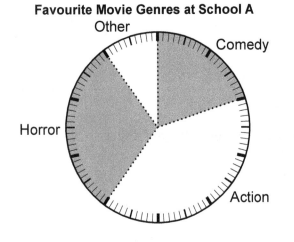

Favourite Movie Genres at School A

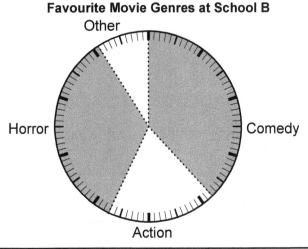

Favourite Movie Genres at School B

	Comedy	Action	Horror	Other	Total
School A	20%	40%			
School B					

b) What is the total percentage for each school? _____ Why does this make sense?

---

5. Diba copied down the following percentages from a circle graph she saw on a website.

Movie Genre	Comedy	Action	Horror	Other
Percentage	22%	37%	18%	25%

How do you know that she made a mistake—or that the website did?

6. Majid and Kim go to different schools. They surveyed the Grade 7 students at their schools about their favourite genres of music.

Music Genre	Classical	Rock	Hip-Hop	Other
Number of Students in Majid's School	10	30	110	50
Number of Students in Kim's School	5	10	20	15

a) How many Grade 7 students did Majid survey?_____ How many did Kim survey?_____

b) Find the fraction of Grade 7 students at each school who likes each type of music. Write the fraction as an equivalent fraction over 100, and then change it to a percentage.

Majid's School

	Fraction	Percentage
Classical	$\dfrac{10}{200}$	$= \dfrac{5}{100} = 5\%$
Rock		
Hip-Hop		
Other		

Kim's School

	Fraction	Percentage
Classical		
Rock		
Hip-Hop		
Other		

c) Complete the circle graphs to show the percentages you calculated in part b).

Favourite Music Genres at Majid's School

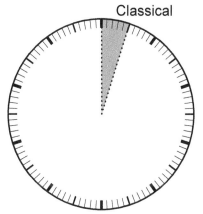

Classical

Favourite Music Genres at Kim's School

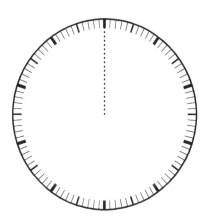

d) More people at Majid's school than at Kim's school like rock music. Explain why your circle graph doesn't show this.

SP7-8 Creating Circle Graphs

REMINDER: A whole circle has 360°. To calculate what central angle is 15% of a circle, find 15% of 360:

$$15\% \text{ of } 360 = \frac{15}{100} \times 360$$

$$= \frac{3}{20} \times 360$$

$$= \frac{3}{2} \times 36 = \frac{108}{2} = 54, \text{ so } 15\% \text{ of a circle is } 54°.$$

1. a) Find the percentage of students who use each mode of transportation to get to school. Then find the central angle of each section in the circle.

How Students Get to School

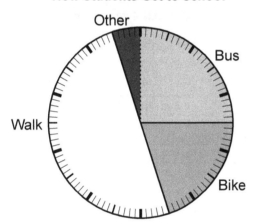

	Percentage	Central Angle in Circle
Bus	25%	$\frac{25}{100} \times 360° = \frac{1}{4} \times 360° = 90°$
Bike	20%	
Walk		
Other		

b) Measure the central angle of the Bus section using a protractor. Can you confirm that 25% of 360° is 90°? _____

c) Add the percentages for all sections.   _____ + _____ + _____ + _____ = _____

Did you get a total of 100%? If not, find your mistake.

d) Add the four central angles.   _____ + _____ + _____ + _____ = _____

Did you get a total of 360°? If not, find your mistake.

A central angle that shows 10% of a circle is $\frac{10}{100} \times 360 = 36°$. Therefore, a central angle that shows 1% of a circle is $36 \div 10 = 3.6°$. A central angle that shows 2% is $2 \times 3.6 = 7.2°$, and so on.

2. Using a calculator, find the central angle for the given percentage of a circle.
   Hint: Use the fact that 1% of a circle is 3.6°.

   a) 5% _5 × 3.6 = 18°_____

   b) 15% _____

   c) 25% _____

   d) 40% _____

   e) 32%_____

   f) 73% _____

3. Complete the chart and then use your protractor to draw a circle graph. You may start your first radius at "noon" and then build the sectors in a clockwise direction. Use labels to make it clear what each part of the circle represents. Make sure that all your percentages total 100% and all your angles total 360°.

a) Survey results: Exercise habits

Title: _____

	Percentage	Central Angle in Circle
Exercises at Home	30%	$30 \times 3.6 = 108°$
Exercises at a Gym	50%	
Never Exercises	20%	

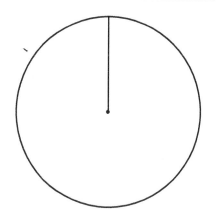

b) Survey results: How students spend money

Title: _____

	Percentage	Central Angle in Circle
Entertainment (Movies, Video Games, etc.)	45%	
Clothing and Personal Care	30%	
Snacks	10%	
Savings	15%	

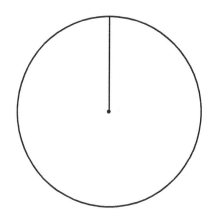

c) Survey results: Favourite kinds of pie

Title: _____

	Percentage	Central Angle in Circle
Apple	20%	
Blueberry	15%	
Cherry	10%	
Other	55%	

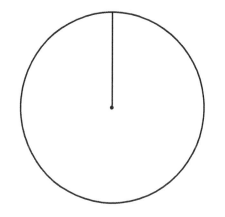

4. Write the fraction as an equivalent fraction over 360 to determine the degree measure (the central angle) in a circle graph.

a) $\dfrac{8}{20} = \dfrac{8 \times 18}{20 \times 18} = \dfrac{144}{360} = 144°$

b) $\dfrac{3}{10} = \dfrac{3 \times}{10 \times 36} = \dfrac{}{360} = °$

c) $\dfrac{13}{40} = \dfrac{13 \times}{40 \times} = \dfrac{}{360} = °$

d) $\dfrac{90}{400} = \dfrac{}{40} = \dfrac{\times}{40 \times} = \dfrac{}{360} = °$

e) $\dfrac{35}{100} = \dfrac{}{20} = \dfrac{\times}{\times} = \dfrac{}{360} = °$

Bonus ▶ $\dfrac{21}{108} =$

5. a) Complete the relative frequency table. Then draw a circle graph using a protractor.

Favourite Sport	Frequency	Fraction of Total	Central Angle
Hockey	8	$\dfrac{8}{20} = \dfrac{144}{360}$	144°
Swimming	5		
Running	4		
Other	3		

Title: _____

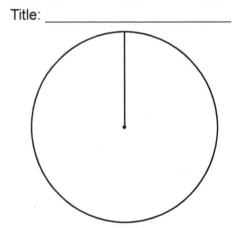

b)

Favourite Sport	Frequency	Fraction of Total	Central Angle
Board games	15		
Card games	8		
Video games	24		
Other	13		

Title: _____

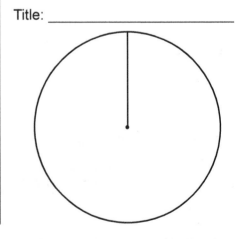

c) Rani says the total frequency in part b) is 60, so you should be able to multiply each frequency by 6 to find the central angle. Is Rani correct? Why or why not?

SP7-9 Interpreting Circle Graphs

1. The percentage of people in each company who work part-time is given.

☐ **Full-time staff**

▨ **Part-time staff**

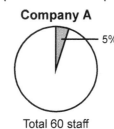

Company A

5%

Total 60 staff

Company B

38%

Total 80 staff

Company C

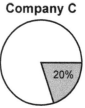

20%

Total 70 staff

a) How many employees in each company work part-time?

Company A   **Company B**   **Company C**

$5\% \text{ of } 60 \text{ is } \dfrac{5}{100} \times 60$

$\dfrac{1}{100} \times 60$

$\dfrac{60}{20} = 3$

Bonus ▶ Use two methods to find the number of full-time employees in Company B.
Hint: Use your answer in part a).

2. The circle graph shows modes of transportation used to get to school for 120 Grade 7 students. Find how many Grade 7 students use each mode of transportation to get to school.

Walk: $35\% \text{ of } 120 = \dfrac{35}{100} \times 120 = \dfrac{7}{20} \times 120 = \dfrac{7}{1} \times 6 = 42$

How Grade 7 Students Get to School

Other 15%

Bus 20%

Walk 35%

Bike 30%

Bike: $30\% \text{ of } 120 =$

Bus: $20\% \text{ of } 120 =$

Other: $15\% \text{ of } 120 =$

3. a) The number of students from two different schools who like each genre of movie is given. Find the percentages.

Favourite Movie Genres at School A

Other 70, Action 50, 20 Horror, 60 Comedy

Favourite Movie Genres at School B

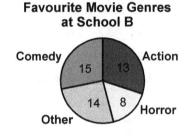

Comedy 15, Action 13, 14 Other, 8 Horror

	Comedy	Horror	Action	Other
School A	$\dfrac{60}{200} = 30\%$			
School B				

b) The Comedy section in both circle graphs is the same size. Why does this make sense?

4. Using a calculator, change the fraction to a decimal (rounded to 3 decimal places) and then to a percentage (rounded to 1 decimal place).

a) $\dfrac{7}{12} \approx 0.\underline{\ 5\ }\ \underline{\ 8\ }\ \underline{\ 3\ } \approx \underline{\ 58.3\ }\%$

b) $\dfrac{8}{15} \approx 0.\underline{\ \ }\ \underline{\ \ }\ \underline{\ \ } \approx \underline{\ \ \ }\%$

c) $\dfrac{7}{18} \approx 0.\underline{\ \ }\ \underline{\ \ }\ \underline{\ \ } \approx \underline{\ \ \ }\%$

d) $\dfrac{5}{36} \approx 0.\underline{\ \ }\ \underline{\ \ }\ \underline{\ \ } \approx \underline{\ \ \ }\%$

Sometimes, the frequency in a circle graph does not correspond to a whole number percentage.

Example: A frequency is 10 out of a total of 120 data points. $\dfrac{10}{120} = 0.08\overline{3}$, so 10 is $8.\overline{3}\%$ of 120.

Usually, we can round the percentage to one decimal place. So we can say that 10 is about 8.3% of 120.

---

5. Using a calculator, write the number as a fraction of the given total. Then find the percentage rounded to one decimal place.

a) 15 out of 90: $\dfrac{15}{90} \approx 0.166 \approx \underline{\ 16.7\ }\%$

b) 100 out of 180: $\dfrac{100}{180} \approx \underline{\ \ \ } \approx \underline{\ \ \ }\%$

c) 1 out of 9: $\dfrac{\boxed{}}{\boxed{}} \approx \underline{\ \ \ } \approx \underline{\ \ \ }\%$

Bonus ▶ 132° of a circle: $\dfrac{\boxed{}}{360} \approx \underline{\ \ \ } \approx \underline{\ \ \ }\%$

6. Meri wants to be on her school's soccer team this year. She decides to do soccer drills for an hour each day. The circle graph shows her data recorded over 30 days.

Time (hours) Meri Spent on Soccer Drills Over 30 Days

a) Add all numbers in the sections. Do you get a total of 30?

b) Find the fraction and use a calculator to find the percentage to one decimal place for each section.

	Dribbling	Passing	Shooting	Juggling	Throw-ins
Fraction	12.5 out of 30 $= \dfrac{125}{300}$	6.25 out of 30 $= \dfrac{}{3000}$			
Percentage	41.7%				

c) Add the percentages. Do you get a total of 100%?

d) Round your answers from part a) to the nearest whole number and add the percentages. Do you get a total of 100%? What happened?

e) Meri can only practise for 24 hours next month. She plans to practise the same percentage of each drill as she did this month. How many hours of each type of drill should she plan to do?

f) The soccer coach at Meri's school has given her a pyramid to show how much of each type of drill she should do each month to make the soccer team. Compare what Meri has done this month to these guidelines. Do you think Meri will make the soccer team?

SP7-10 Mean

To find a mean of a set of data, such as 5, 2, 2, 5, 6:

Step 1: Add the data values. $5 + 2 + 2 + 5 + 6 = 20$

Step 2: Divide the sum by the number of data values. $20 \div 5 = 4$

Mean = sum of data values $\div$ number of data values

1. Find the mean.

	Data Set	Sum of Data Values	Number of Data Values	Mean
a)	9 5	$9 + 5 = 14$	2	$14 \div 2 = 7$
b)	7 7 7 7 7			
c)	5 14 8 11 2 8			
d)	18 0 12 −10			
e)	100 500 300 100			

Some means will not be whole numbers.

f)	3.2 2.9 2.8 3.5			
g)	8.35 11.95 5 8.2 12.3			

2. Kate's marks on some math quizzes were 7, 9, and 8. She missed one quiz.

   a) If the teacher does not count the quiz Kate missed, what is the mean of her marks? _____

   b) If the teacher counts the quiz Kate missed as 0, what is the mean of her marks? _____

   c) Which option, a) or b), is better for Kate? Explain.

3. Use the data set 4, 6, 6, 6, 7, 7 to answer the question.

   a) Find the sum of the data values. _____ + _____ + _____ + _____ + _____ + _____ = _____

   b) Write how many times each data value occurs. Then finish the calculation.

      (_____ × 4) + (_____ × 6) + (_____ × 7) = _____ + _____ + _____ = _____

   c) Did you get the same answer in parts a) and b)? If not, find your mistake.

   d) Find the mean. _____ ÷ _____ = _____

4. Use multiplication and addition to total the data values. Then find the mean.

   a) 2, 2, 2, 4, 4, 8, 3, 3, 3, 9   b) 5, 5, 3, 3, 5, 5, 3, 5, 5, 3   c) 500, 500, 300, 300, 500

5. Alexa studies mallard ducks. She made a table showing the number of eggs (the clutch size) in the nests she found.

Clutch Size	Number of Nests	Total Number of Eggs
9	4	*36*
10	6	
11	4	
12	0	
13	1	

    a) Fill in the table.

    b) Find the average (mean) size of the mallard clutches.

        _____ ÷ _____ = _____

    c) Alexa finds another nest. It has 11 eggs.

        Is that nest larger than average? _____

    d) If Alexa adds this nest to the data, how will the mean change? Predict, then check your prediction.

        Predict:

        Check:

6. The table shows Carl's marks in three subjects, out of 100.

English	76, 89, 85, 87, 90, 85, 90
French	81, 90, 90, 86, 93, 90, 70, 88
Math	70, 77, 83, 80, 85, 78, 77, 80, 80, 100

    a) Find the mean mark for each subject.

    b) In which subject does Carl do best?

    c) Carl thinks he does better in French than in English because he has more 90s in French than in English. Do you agree? Does the mean show this? Explain.

    d) Carl thinks math is his strongest subject because it is the only subject in which he got a 100 mark. Do you agree? Does the mean show this? Explain.

7. a) Find the mean of the data set 2, 3, 6, 9.

    b) Add 4 to each data value in part a) to get the data set 6, 7, 10, 13. What is the mean of the new data set? How does it compare to the mean of the original data set?

    c) Construct a data set from 2, 3, 6, 9 that has a mean of 7.

    d) Find the mean of the data set 2, 2, 3, 3, 6, 6, 9, 9. How was this new data set obtained from the original data set? How does the mean of the new data set compare to the mean of the original data set?

    e) Predict and check the mean of the data set 2, 2, 2, 3, 3, 3, 6, 6, 6, 9, 9, 9.

SP7-11 Measures of Central Tendency

To find the **median** of a set of data, put the data in order from lowest to highest. Count from either end until you reach the centre.

2   3   ⑥   7   11
The median is 6.

2   3   ⑦   ⑨   11   15
The median is 8, halfway between 7 and 9.

1. a) Find the mean and the median.

   i) 9   20   22

   Mean: _(9 + 20 + 22) ÷ 3_

   _= 51 ÷ 3 = 17_

   Median: _20_

   ii) 38   39   41   46

   Mean: _____

   _____

   Median: _____

   iii) 10   15   20   25   30

   Mean: _____

   _____

   Median: _____

   b) Order the numbers from lowest to highest, then find the mean and the median. Show your work.

   i) 15   18   40   32   25

   _____

   Mean:

   Median:

   ii) 29   26   16   23   17   15

   _____

   Mean:

   Median:

   iii) 40   25   10   15   20

   _____

   Mean:

   Median:

2. When finding the median, does it matter whether you write the data values from lowest to highest or from highest to lowest? Explain.

3. a) Find the mean and median of the data.

   b) Describe how the mean changes as the last data value increases.

Data Set					Median	Mean
1	1	2	5	6	2	3
1	1	2	5	11	2	4
1	1	2	5	16		
1	1	2	5	21		

   c) Describe how the median changes as the last data value increases.

4. In 2008, the population of the United States was 307 million people, and the country's electricity consumption was 4 401 698 gigawatt-hours per year (GWh/yr). Canada's population in 2008 was 33 million and the country's electricity consumption was 620 684 GWh/yr. Which country used more electricity per person in 2008?

5. Arsham wrote 5 science tests and 8 math tests last year. Here are his results: Science: 82, 79, 75, 84, 80; Math: 75, 81, 77, 86, 79, 80, 83, 82. In which subject did he do better? Hint: Find the mean for each subject.

6. a) The mean of a data set is 10. The data values are 2, 19, 7, 4, 15, and one other number. Let x represent the missing number. Write an expression for the mean, and then solve the equation.

   b) If your marks were 81, 94, and 92 on your first three history tests, what do you need to get on the next test to average 91 on the first four history tests?

   Bonus ▶ Is it possible to get an average of 93 for the first four history quizzes? Explain.

   The **mode** of a set of data is the most common data value. The mode of the set 1, 2, 2, 2, 3, 4, 4 is 2.

7. There are 20 employees at Company XYZ. One person has a salary of $200 000, two people have salaries of $88 000, and the rest have salaries of $32 000.

   a) What is the mean salary?

   b) What is the median salary?

   c) Which reflects the salaries in the company better, the mean or the median? Explain.

   d) The company says that they are bringing well-paying jobs to the community because the average salary is above $45 000. Is that correct? Use the mode and the median in your explanation.

SP7-12 Outliers

The **range** of a data set is the difference between the highest and the lowest values in the data set.

range = highest value − lowest value

Example: The range of the data set 9, 5, 8, 5, 11, 8, 7, 8, 10 is 6, because 11 − 5 = 6.

1. The set shows the temperature (°C) for one week in the summer and one week in the winter. Find the range.

	Sun	Mon	Tues	Wed	Thu	Fri	Sat
a)	31	28	33	22	27	26	29
b)	−7	−11	−14	−9	−8	−6	−10

Range: _____ − _____ = _____

Range: _____ − _____ = _____

c) Put all data values in parts a) and b) together and find the range of the new data set

with 14 data values. Range: _____ − _____ = _____

2. a) Find the mean, mode, median, and range for the data set: 8, 5, 7, 5, 2, 3.

Mean: _____   Mode: _____

Median: _____   Range: _____

b) Add 10 to each data value and find the new mean, median, and range.

Mean: _____

Median: _____   Range: _____

c) How did the mean and median change after you added 10 to each data value? _____

d) Did the range change when you added 10 to each data value? _____

3. a) Find the mean, median, mode, and range for each data set.

Data Set	Mean	Median	Mode	Range
A: 10, 10, 10, 10, 10, 10, 10, 10, 10				
B: 1, 10, 10, 10, 10, 10, 10, 10, 19				
C: 1, 2, 9, 10, 10, 10, 11, 18, 19				

b) Does the mean, median, or mode best show the differences among these sets? _____

c) Does the range help you to compare data set A and data set B? _____ What does it tell you?

d) Does the range help you to compare data set B and data set C? _____ How so?

4. Create a set of data with the given median and range. You can use the same value.
more than once in a set.

a) Median: 7, Range: 3   Set: _____, _____, _____, _7_, _____, _____, _____

b) Median: 7, Range: 8   Set: _____, _____, _____, _____, _____, _____, _____

5. Consider the set 8, 5, 2, 7, 64.

a) What is the range of the set? _____

b) Remove one value from the set and find the range of the new set. Repeat with all other values.

New set: _5_, _2_, _7_, _64_   Range: _64 − 2 = 62_ _____

New set: _____, _____, _____, ____   Range: _____

New set: _____, _____, _____, ____   Range: _____

New set: _____, _____, _____, ____   Range: _____

New set: _____, _____, _____, ____   Range: _____

c) Removing which data value has the most effect on the range? _____

An **outlier** is a data value that is far from the rest of the data values in the set. Removing an outlier changes the range of the set by a lot.

Example: In the set 2, 3, 4, 5, 90, the number 90 is the outlier.

---

6. Consider the set 2, 3, 3, 4, 5, 73.

a) Circle the outlier.

b) Find the mean, median, and mode of the set.

c) Write the set without the outlier: _____, _____, _____, _____, _____. Find the mean, median, and mode of the new set.

d) Which one was changed the most by the removal of the outlier: the mean, median, or mode?

e) Remove the data value closest to the outlier and write the set without it:

_____, _____, _____, _____, 76. Find the mean, median, and mode of the new set.

f) What affects the mean more: the removal of the outlier or the removal of another value?

g) When there are outliers, is it better to use the mean or median to describe the data set? _____

SP7-13 When to Include Outliers in Reporting

REMINDER: An outlier is a value that is very different from the other values in the set.

1. The set 1, 3, 4, 4 does not have an outlier.

   a) Find the mean, median, mode, and the range of the data set.

   Mean: _____

   Median: _____   Mode: _____   Range: _____

   b) If you add 100 to the data set as a new data value, what will be affected more:

   the mean, median, or mode? _____ Check your prediction.

   New mean: _____

   New median: _____   New mode: _____   New range: _____

2. This set does not have an outlier: 2, 3, 4, 100, 102, 103. Explain why none of the data values are outliers.

An outlier influences the mean and range. Removing it from the data set can change the mean and range significantly. Sometimes you need to decide when an outlier should or shouldn't be included. Sometimes an outlier is an error. Sometimes it is simply unusual.

3. a) Circle the outlier in each set of data.

   A. Ages of the members of the bridge club in Golden Age Retirement Residence:

   68, 76, 78, 84, 91, 69, 7, 69, 75, 84, 77

   B. Yearly salaries of employees in a company: $35 000, $38 000, $7000, $40 000

   C. Hourly rate of contract workers in a company: $25, $17.50, $3000, $45

   b) In which of the situations in part a) is the outlier likely a mistake in the data and shouldn't be included? _____ Explain.

4. Emily records the ages of campers in the group she is responsible for at a summer camp:

   6, 7, 7, 6, 77, 6, 7. Should the outlier be included in the calculations of the mean or median? _____

   Why or why not?

5. The panel of judges for a school talent show includes three teachers and one student representative from each grade. Josh is performing in the competition and his best friend is one of the judges. Josh's marks from the judges out of 10 are: 3, 4, 3, 5, 3, 4, 3, 4, 10, 3, 3. Should the outlier be included when calculating Josh's average mark? Explain why.

6. At a school fundraiser, the following amounts of money (in dollars) were raised by each grade: 150, 130, 127, 854, 99, 112.50, 154, 167. To find the average amount of money raised per grade, should the outlier be included? Why or why not?

7. The average weight of three dogs, Tippy, Pat, and Baxter, is 25 kg. Tippy weighs 41 kg. Pat and Baxter both weigh the same amount.

   a) What is Pat's weight?

   b) Is there an outlier in the data set of dog weights? _____

   c) Should you include the outlier in the calculation of the average? _____

8. Celine's math test marks (out of 20) are 16, 17, 17, 5, 19, 18, 17, 20, and 19.

   a) Find the mean: _____

   b) What is the outlier in this set? _____

   c) Remove the outlier and find the mean of the new set. _____

   d) Why might Celine's teacher decide to remove this outlier when calculating the average for Celine's report card?

9. A one-day filming shoot for a movie was filmed outside 10 Portage Street. A small coffee shop sits at 8 Portage Street. Its sales for the day were 1000 times greater than any other day that year.

   a) Will the data set of the daily sales for the year contain an outlier? _____

   b) To keep track of sales, the coffee shop finds the average daily sales for the year.

      Should the owners of the shop include the outlier in the calculation? _____

   c) The owners decide to sell the store. They want to include the average daily sales in an advertisement. Should they include the outlier in the calculation of the average? Explain.

SP7-14 Choosing a Measure of Central Tendency

1. You work at a clothing store, and your manager says that every week you need to sell an average of at least $500. What kind of average do you think your manager is talking about: the mean, mode, or median? Why?

2. A Grade 8 student needs to average at least 85% to get into a high school that has a Digital Arts program. Which average do you think this is referring to: the mean, median, or mode? Why?

3. A karate school will allow you to pass the test for the next belt if you score more than 70 on at least half of the tests and have an average of at least 75.

   a) Which averages are used here and what are their values? _____

   b) Is the third type of average useful here? Explain.

4. The table shows the price for the same pair of pants at seven different stores.

Store	A	B	C	D	E	F	G
Price ($)	83	85	84	86	86	82	81

   a) Store B claims that its prices are lower than average. Which average could they use to make this statement true: the mean, mode, or median? _____

   b) Do you think the claim is misleading? Why or why not?

5. You are going on a trip during the spring break and need to decide what kind of clothes you should pack. The data shows the highest daily temperatures (in degrees Celsius) at your destination during spring break last year.

Day	1	2	3	4	5	6	7	8	9	10	11	12	13	14	15
Temp. (°C)	23	22	20	21	22	23	23	10	2	2	5	7	8	12	17

   a) Find the range, mean, median, and mode of the temperatures.

   b) What does the range of temperatures tell you about what you should pack?

   c) If you looked only at the mode of the temperatures, what mistake might you make in your packing?

6. Suppose you are a manager for a shoe company. A famous, big-league athlete has agreed to autograph just one shoe for the store. You want it to be an average shoe size so that as many customers as possible can try on the shoe. Which average shoe size should you consider: the mean, the median, or the mode? _____ Why?

7. The data shows the class marks on a test:

   76, 78, 69, 76, 73, 76, 74, 66, 69, 85, 74, 66, 71, 76, 87, 96, 66, 98, 91, 73

   a) Find the range, mode, median, and mean of the data.

   b) Tom's mark was 76. Is the statement that he told his parents true or false? Explain using the mean, mode, median, or range.

      i)   I did better than half of the class!   True / False

           Why?

      ii) My grade is higher than the average!   True / False

           Why?

      iii) A lot of students had the same grade as me. True / False

           Why?

      iv) Only 6 students got a better mark than me!   True / False

           Why?

      v)   76 was the most common mark.   True / False

           Why?

8. a) Find the mean and the median of the sets.

      Set A: 2, 3, 4   Set B: 2, 3, 4, 5, 6

   b) Move one data value from set A to set B. Find the mean and the median of the new sets. Did the mean and the median of each set increase, decrease, or stay the same?

   c) Explain why the mean and the median of set B cannot increase if any single data value from set A is added.

SP7-15 Problems and Puzzles with Data

1. Sohara surveys 20 families in her apartment building
   to find the number of cats they have.
   She displays the results in a circle graph.

   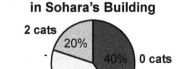

   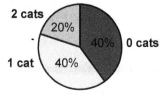

   Number of Cats Families Have
   in Sohara's Building

   a) Find the mode and the median of the data.

   Mode: _____   Median: _____

   b) How many families have no cat? _____

   c) How many families have two cats? _____

   d) Find the mean of the data.

2. The circle graph shows the percentage of people in a small
   island nation earning various annual (yearly) incomes.

   a) Use the circle graph to find the mean, median, and
      mode. Hint: Pretend the country has only 100 people.

   Annual Incomes in a
   Small Island Nation

   Between $5000 ⌐ ⌐ $40 000 or more
   and $40 000   (1%)
   (4%)

   Less than $5000
   (95%)

   b) Explain why you do not need to know the population of
      the country to determine the mean salary.

   c) If you were studying this country and wanted to decide if the average citizen
      had an income that they could live on, which average would you look at:

      the median, mode, or mean? _____

      Explain.

3. a) Jamshid has 3 apples, Lily has 5 apples, and Reza has 10 apples. If they want to
      share the apples equally, how many apples should Reza give Jamshid and Lily?

   b) Find the mean of the data set 3, 5, and 10. How is your answer related to part a)?

   c) Beth has six apples. Does she have to give any apples to Reza, Jamshid, or Lily
      for the apples to be shared equally among the four people? Do any of the others
      have to give apples to Beth? Explain.

4. The mean of the ages of all of Fernando's cousins is 10. Five of the cousins are 3, 18, 6, 4, and 15 years old. Two other cousins have the same age. Let x represent the missing age. Write the expression for the mean and solve the equation.

5. a) If you got 80, 93, and 91 on your first three history tests, what do you need to get on the next one to average at least 90 on your first four history tests?

   b) Dylan wants an average of 85 in Geography class. His marks on the first five tests are 72, 86, 92, 73, and 76. There is just one more test. Can he do it? Explain.

6. Create a data set with four data values that has a mode of 8, a median of 9, and a mean of 10.

7. When a volleyball player moved from Team A to Team B, the mean age of both teams increased. Create two sets of data to show how this could happen.

8. Roz went to the local museum for an archaeology summer camp. To help in a study, she weighed some ancient coins. The table shows her record of the number of ancient coins of various weights.

Weight (g)	5	6	7	11	12	17	120
Frequency	8	6	5	1	2	2	1

   a) Find the mean and the median.

   b) Calculate what the mean and the median would be if the outlier was 70 instead of 120.

   c) Calculate what the mean and the median would be if the outlier was 320 instead of 120.

   d) Does changing the value of the outlier change the mean and the median? _____

   e) Predict: if you remove the outlier, will the mean and median increase or decrease? _____

   f) Remove the outlier and then find the mean and median.

   g) Explain why only the mean changed when you left out the outlier.

1. Complete the table.

Expression	$-12t - 29$	$72 - 21B$	$x - 123$	$5h$
Variable Term	$-12t$			
Variable	t			
Coefficient	-12			
Constant Term	-29			

2. Solve for the variable by applying opposite operations to both sides of the equation. Show each step.

a) $39n = 13$

$$\frac{39n}{39} = \frac{13}{39}$$

$$n = \frac{13}{39} = \frac{1}{3}$$

b) $25x - 31 = 194$

c) $\frac{b}{8} + 15 = 21$

3. Francisco is going on a road trip. They drive at a speed of 90 km per hour. They make two stops, the first for 10 minutes and the second for 20 minutes. The trip takes a total of 4 hours. What distance does Francisco travel?

4. Sue is 3 times as old as her daughter. Sue's older sister is 46. The difference between Sue's and her older sister's age is 4 years. How old is Sue's daughter?

5. Find the area and the distance around the shape.

a)

b)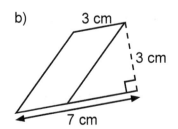

4 cm

8 cm

Bonus ▶ Find the area of the parallelogram.

a)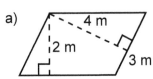

4 m

2 m

3 m

b) 3 cm

3 cm

7 cm

6. A van has six windows: 4 rectangles and 2 parallelograms. The height of all six windows is 1 m and the width (base) is 1.4 m. Glass costs $37 for each 1 m². How much will it cost to replace the glass in all six windows?

7. A bike wheel has a diameter of 60 cm. About how many times would the wheel turn if the bike drove 1 km?

8. Will the fraction convert into a terminating or repeating decimal?

a) $\dfrac{37}{148}$

b) $\dfrac{20}{72}$

Bonus ▶ $\dfrac{9}{8411}$

9. Ava's meal at a restaurant is $23 before taxes. The tax is 12%. Ava also wants to leave a tip of 15% of the cost of the meal before taxes. How much will she pay in total?

10. Farah spent one hour doing homework. The chart shows the time they spent on each subject. Complete the chart.

Subject	Fraction of 1 Hour	Percentage of 1 Hour	Decimal	Number of Minutes
English	$\dfrac{1}{5}$		0.2	12
Science	$\dfrac{1}{10}$	10%		
Math		45%		
French			0.25	

11. A coin is tossed. Then a regular six-sided die is rolled.

a) Use a chart to show the possible outcomes.

b) Find the probability of tossing a head and rolling an even number.

12. A pair of dice is rolled 180 times. Predict the number of times the total will be 9.

13. Explain why the theoretical probability and experimental probability will usually not be the same.

14. Draw an obtuse angle. Construct the bisector of the angle you constructed using different methods.

    a) Use a protractor and a ruler.   b) Use a ruler only.

    c) Use a compass and a straightedge.   d) Explain why the line you constructed in parts b) and c) bisects your angle.

15. a) Use a protractor and a ruler or a set square to construct a line *m* that is parallel to the line *l* through the point *P*.

    b) Explain how you know that line *m* is parallel to line *l*.

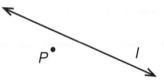

16. Complete the relative frequency table. Then draw a circle graph using a protractor.

Favourite Book Type	Frequency	Fraction of total	Central Angle
Classic	35	$\dfrac{35}{90} = \dfrac{}{360}$	°
Horror	12		
Comic	24		
Other	19		

Title: _____

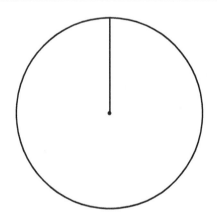

17. The circle graph shows the number of cars for 140 families in a neighbourhood.

    a) Find the mode and the median of the data.

    b) How many families have 2 cars?

    c) How many families have 3 cars?

    Bonus ▶ Find the mean (the average number of cars for each family) using two methods.

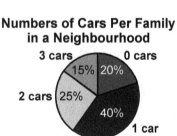

18. Find the mean, median, mode, and range for the data set 17, 19, 22, 17, 45.

    a) Remove the outlier and find the mean, median, mode, and range again.

    b) Which one was changed the most by the removal of the outlier: the mean, median, or mode?

    c) What can you tell about the removal of the outlier on range?

SS7-30 Introduction to Rectangular Prism Volume

Volumo ic tho amount of cpaco takon up by a three-dimensional object.

We measure volume in unit cubes or cubic units.

This object, made of cubic metres, has a volume of 4 m³.

1 om³ — 1 oubio ocntimctro   1 m³ — 1 oubio mctro

1 cm
1 cm
1 cm

1 m
1 m
1 m

1. Find the volume of the object made from unit cubes. Include units in your answer.

a)

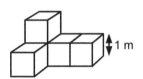

1 m

Volume = ___5 m³___

b)

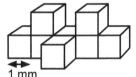

1 mm

Volume = _____

c)

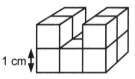

1 cm

Volume = _____

When a 3-D object is made up of identical layers of unit cubes, you can use multiplication to find the volume of the object.

2. Blocks are stacked to make these boxes.

 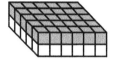

a) How many blocks are in the shaded layer?   ___4 × 2 = 8___   _____   _____

b) How many blocks are in each layer?   ___8___   _____   _____

c) How many horizontal layers are there?   ___3___   _____   _____

d) How many blocks in the whole box?   ___3 × 8 = 24___   _____   _____

e) If each block is a cubic centimetre, what is the volume of the box?   ___24 cm³___   _____   _____

f) If each block is a cubic metre, what is the volume of the box?   ___24 m³___   _____   _____

Bonus ▶ Each block is a cubic millimetre. Find the volume of the object. Show your work.

a)

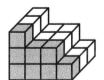

b)

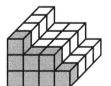

c)

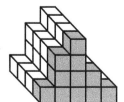

_____   _____   _____

Remember, mathematicians call rectangular boxes "rectangular prisms." A rectangular prism can be divided into identical layers of unit cubes. The volume of the prism is the volume of one layer multiplied by the number of identical layers.

3. Draw lines connecting the tick marks to show how to divide the prism into unit cubes. Use a ruler.

a)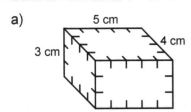

b)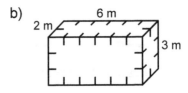

4. The rectangular prism is divided into identical layers of unit cubes.

   a) Find the volume of the shaded layer.

   i)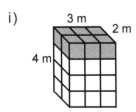

   ii)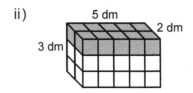

   iii)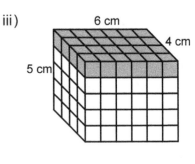

   i) $\underline{\quad 3 \times 2 = 6 \; m^3 \quad}$

   ii) _____

   iii) _____

   b) Use the volume of the shaded layer to find the volume of the prism.

   i) $\underline{\quad 4 \times 6 = 24 \; m^3 \quad}$

   ii) _____

   iii) _____

Bonus ▶ A rectangular prism is divided into cubic millimetres. The volume of the bottom layer is 180 mm³. There are 100 layers. What is the volume of the prism?

5. Each cube is 1 mm³.

   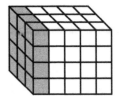

   a) Write a multiplication equation to find the number of blocks in the shaded vertical layer. _____

   b) What is the volume of the shaded layer? _____

   c) How many identical vertical layers are there in the prism? _____

   d) Write a multiplication equation to find the volume of the prism. _____

SS7-31 Formulas for Rectangular Prism Volume

Prisms are 3 D objects that have two identical opposite faces called **bases**.
The other faces are called **side faces**. All faces are polygons.

Prisms are named by the shape of their bases.

Examples:

triangular prism   rectangular prism   pentagonal prism

The bases are shaded. Hidden edges are shown with dashed lines.

1. a) Shade one base of the prism. Then name the prism.

i)   ii)   iii)

_____   _____   _____

b) What shape are the side faces? _____

c) How many side faces does the prism have?

i) _____   ii) _____   iii) _____

Aki puts two prisms on a table. They are not exactly alike.

In a **right prism**, the side faces are rectangles and the top base is
directly above the bottom base.

In a **skew prism**, the side faces are parallelograms and the top
base is not directly above the bottom base.

2. Shade a base of the prism. Is the prism right or skew?

 a)   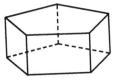   b) 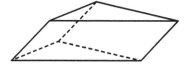   c)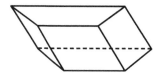

_____   _____   _____

d) 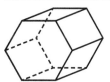   e) 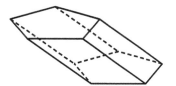   f)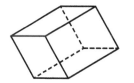

_____   _____   _____

The height of a prism is the distance between its two bases. The height matches the vertical dimension only when one base is the bottom face.

3. Circle the measurement that gives the height of the prism. Hint: Shade the two bases.

a)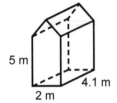

5 m
4.1 m
2 m

b)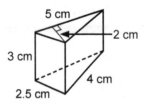

5 cm
2 cm
3 cm
4 cm
2.5 cm

c)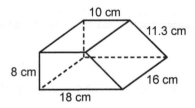

10 cm
11.3 cm
8 cm
16 cm
18 cm

In a rectangular prism, any pair of opposite faces can be the bases. The choice of the bases determines the height of the prism.

4. One of the bases is shaded. Circle the height of the prism.

a)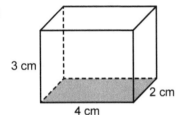

3 cm
2 cm
4 cm

b)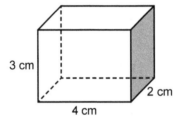

3 cm
2 cm
4 cm

c)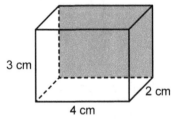

3 cm
2 cm
4 cm

The three dimensions (length, width, and height) of a rectangular prism can be labelled in different ways.

5. The shaded face is a base. The height is the distance between the two bases. Fill in the blanks. Let the length be the longer of the other two dimensions.

a)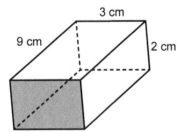

3 cm
9 cm
2 cm

height = _____

length = _____

width = _____

b)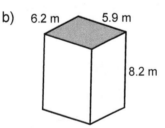

6.2 m
5.9 m
8.2 m

height = _____

length = _____

width = _____

c)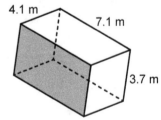

4.1 m
7.1 m
3.7 m

height = _____

length = _____

width = _____

6. In Question 5, what is the vertical dimension of the prism? Does it match the height of the prism?

a) _____

b) _____

c) _____

Ezra places a rectangular prism built of cubic centimetres on a table, resting on its base.

The top layer of cubes is shaded.
This shows the volume of one layer.

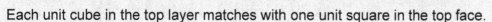

The top faces of the top layer of cubes are shaded.
This shows the area of the top base.

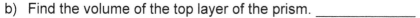

Each unit cube in the top layer matches with one unit square in the top face.

The volume of the top layer is $4 \times 5 = $ **20 cm³**.   The area of the top face is $4 \times 5 = $ **20 cm²**.

7. a) Find the area of the top base of the prism. _____

2 m

   b) Find the volume of the top layer of the prism. _____

   c) Compare your answers to parts a) and b). What is the same? What is different?

8. a) The rectangles, divided into centimetre squares, are each the top face of one of the prisms.
      Match the top face with its corresponding prism.

A.

B.
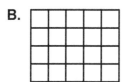

C.
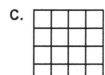

D.
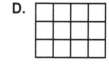

i)
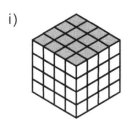

ii)
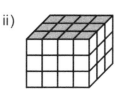

iii)
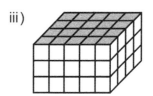

iv)
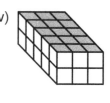

_____   _____   _____   _____

   b) What is the area of the top face of each prism in part a)?

     i) ___$4 \times 4 = 16 \text{ cm}^2$___ ii) _____ iii) _____ iv) _____

   c) What is the volume of the top layer of each prism in part a)?

     i) ___$4 \times 4 = 16 \text{ cm}^3$___ ii) _____ iii) _____ iv) _____

9. Divya says that for any rectangular prism, the area of the top face is the same as the
   volume of a horizontal layer. Do you agree? Explain.

The height of a prism tells you how many layers of cubes are in the prism.

10. Fill in the table. All measurements are in metres. The shaded face is a base.

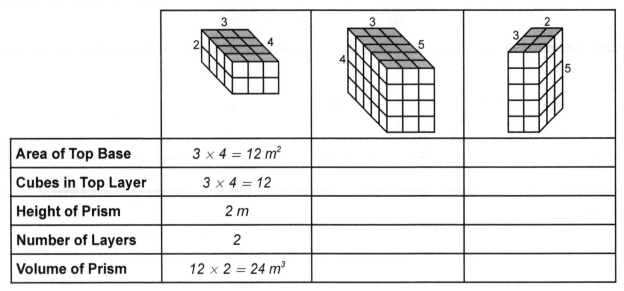

Area of Top Base	$3 \times 4 = 12\ m^2$		
Cubes in Top Layer	$3 \times 4 = 12$		
Height of Prism	$2\ m$		
Number of Layers	2		
Volume of Prism	$12 \times 2 = 24\ m^3$		

11. Write a formula for the volume of a rectangular prism using "area of base" and "height."

Volume = _____

For a rectangular prism: Volume = area of base × height

OR   Volume = length × width × height   OR $V = \ell \times w \times h$

12. Find the volume of the rectangular prism. Include units in your final answer.

a) $\ell =$ _____

  $w =$ _____

  $h =$ _____

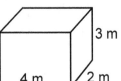

  $V =$ _____

   = _____

b)

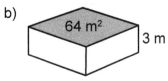

  Volume = _____ × _____

   = _____

The formulas for the volume of a rectangular prism work no matter which face is chosen as a base. The formulas work even if the dimensions are not whole numbers

13. a) A building is a rectangular prism with length 40 m and width 30.5 m. The total volume of the building is 79 422 m³. How tall is the building?

   Bonus ▶ A second building has the same height and length as the building in part a), but its volume is 82 026 m³. How wide is the second building?

SS7-32 Volume of Cylinders

REMINDER: The diameter of a circle is twice the radius: $d = 2r$
The radius of a circle is half the diameter: $r = d \div 2$
The area of a circle with radius r is $A = \pi(r \times r)$. Use 3.14 for π.

1. Find the radius of the circle. Then find the area. Round to the nearest tenth.

a) 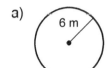 $r =$ _____
   $A \approx$ _____
   $\approx$ _____

b)  $r =$ _____
   $A \approx$ _____
   $\approx$ _____

c) $r =$ _____
   $A \approx$ _____
   $\approx$ _____

Cylinders are 3-D shapes that have:

• two opposite faces that are identical circles
• one curved surface called its side face

The height of a cylinder is the distance between the bases.

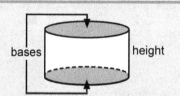

2. Shade the visible base of the cylinder.

a)

b)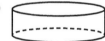

c)

You can describe a cylinder by giving two dimensions:
the height (h) of the cylinder and the radius (r) or diameter (d) of the base.

Examples:

 2 cm
The cylinder has
$r = 2$ cm and $h = 5$ cm.
5 cm

8 m
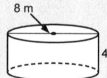 4 m The cylinder has
$d = 8$ m and $h = 4$ m.

3. Identify the dimensions of the cylinder.

a) 3 cm
6 cm

$r =$ _____
$d =$ _____
$h =$ _____

b) 1 mm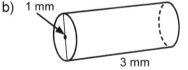
3 mm

$r =$ _____
$d =$ _____
$h =$ _____

c) 4.5 m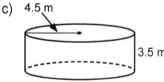
3.5 m

$r =$ _____
$d =$ _____
$h =$ _____

A cylinder is like a prism: you can break it into identical layers. If you know the total number of unit cubes (including partial cubes) in one layer, you can find the volume:

Volume = volume of one layer × number of layers

Each unit cube (and partial unit cube) in the shaded layer corresponds to a square (or partial square) in the base.

So, Volume = area of base × height   OR $V = Ah$

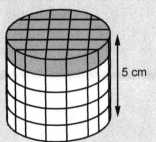

The height tells you the number of layers.

5 cm

4. Find the volume of the cylinder. Include units in the final answer.

a)   16 m² $V =$ ___Ah___

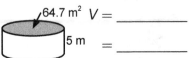

3 m

$= $ ___(16)(3)___

$= $ ___48 m³___

b)   64.7 m² $V =$ _____

5 m

$= $ _____

$= $ _____

c)   22.5 cm²

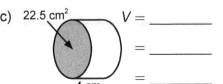

4 cm

$V =$ _____

$= $ _____

$= $ _____

If a cylinder has radius r and height h, the area of its base is $A = \pi(r \times r)$ and its volume is

    $V = A \times h$ or $V = \pi(r \times r)h$

5. Find the volume of the cylinder. Round to the nearest tenth.

a)   8 cm

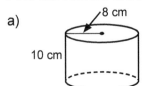

10 cm

$V =$ ___$\pi(r \times r)h$___

$\approx $ ___$3.14(8 \times 8)(10)$___

$= $ ___2009.6 cm³___

b)   20 mm

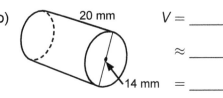

14 mm

$V =$ _____

$\approx $ _____

$= $ _____

c)   1.5 m

8 m

$V =$ _____

$\approx $ _____

$\approx $ _____

d)   10 dm

4 dm

$V =$ _____

$\approx $ _____

$= $ _____

6. A large drinking straw is shaped like a cylinder with radius 3 mm. The total volume of the straw is 5562 mm³. How tall is the straw?

7. a) The inside of a pot is a cylinder with diameter 21 cm. A chef fills the pot to the top with 4154.22 cm³ of water. What is the inside height of the pot?

    Bonus ▶ A second pot has the same height but its radius is 0.5 cm longer. How much water can it hold, to the nearest whole number of cubic centimetres?

SS7-33 Problems and Puzzles: Volume

1. A flat sheet of cardboard is bent and folded along the dashed lines. The two short edges are then joined to form the side faces of a rectangular prism.

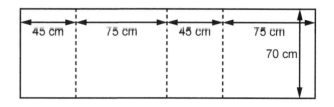

   a) What are the length and width of the base of the resulting rectangular prism?

   _____

   b) What is the height of the prism? _____

   c) Find the volume of the prism.

   Bonus ▶ How could you find the perimeter of the rectangular base without folding the sheet of cardboard?

REMINDER: The circumference of a circle and diameter are related: $C = \pi d$ and $d = C \div \pi$

---

2. a) Fold a standard (22 cm by 28 cm) sheet of paper into a tube in two ways:

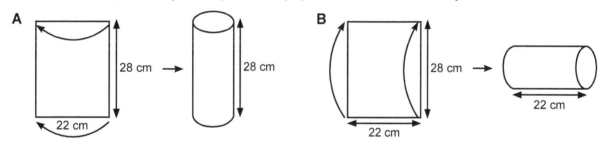

   b) Predict which tube will have the larger volume, Tube A or Tube B. _____

   c) What is the circumference of each tube?   Tube A: $C =$ _____   Tube B: $C =$ _____

   d) Calculate the volume of each tube.

   Tube A: $d = C \div \pi$ Tube B:
   $\approx 22 \div 3.14$
   $\approx 7\ cm$
   $r \approx$

   $h = 28\ cm$
   $V = \pi(r \times r)h$
   $\approx$

   e) Was your prediction in part b) correct? _____

Convert all measurements as necessary before substituting into formulas.

$1\ m = 100\ cm$ $1\ mL = 1\ cm^3$ $1\ L = 1000\ mL$

3. Bilal says the volume of this box is 40 cm³.

   a) Is Bilal correct? Explain.

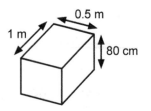

   b) Change the measurements of the box into centimetres and then find the volume.

4. A railway car is a cylinder with diameter 326 cm. It is 17.4 m long. What is its volume in cubic metres? Round your answer to two decimal places.

5. A juice carton in the shape of a rectangular prism holds 2 L. It is 25 cm tall. What is the inside area of the base of the carton?

6. Denali makes a bentwood box using the flat sheet shown. They steam and bend the wood along three lines to make the base a square.

   a) What is the perimeter of the square base of the box they make?

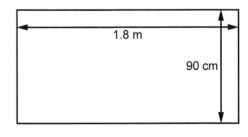

   b) What are the dimensions of the base? _____

   c) What is the height of the inside of the box? _____

   d) Find the volume of the box in cubic centimetres.

Bonus ▶ A sheet of birch bark has the same measurements as the flat sheet in Question 6. Denali rolls it so that the two 90 cm edges touch, forming a tube. What is the volume of this tube in cubic centimetres? Round your answer to the nearest thousand.

7. The two containers shown hold the same amount of soup. How tall is the second container?

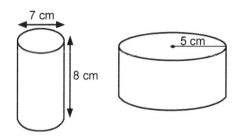

8. Rayla has the two containers shown. All measurements are inside measurements.

a) Predict which container will hold more. _____

b) Calculate the volume of each container. Which one holds more?

Container A: Container B:

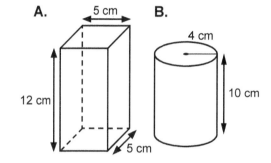

c) Rayla fills the cylinder with water. Explain how she can check which container will hold more without first finding the volume of each.

9. a) Each dimension of the larger juice box is twice the corresponding dimension of the smaller juice box. Write the dimensions of the larger box.

b) Find the volume of each juice box.

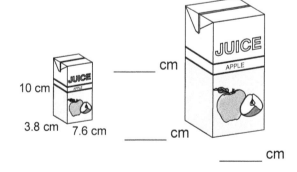

Bonus ▶ The small juice box costs $0.50. How much should the large juice box cost if the price per millilitre is the same for both boxes? Show your work and explain your answer.